Berlitz®

Stockholm

Front cover: Gamla Stan

Right: Three golden crowns
cap the Stadshuset

Skansen • Step into Sweden's past at the open-air museum *(page 53)*

Drottningholm Palace • Described as the Versailles of Sweden *(page 70)*

Stadshuset • The City Hall dominates Stockholm's skyline *(page 41)*

Uppsala • A rewarding excursion from Stockholm *(page 77)*

Hallwylska Museet • A patrician mansion displaying over 70,000 objects *(page 58)*

Vasamuseet • The permanent home of the 17th-century Vasa warship *(page 50)*

Nationalmuseum • Sweden's largest art collection *(page 44)*

Moderna Museet • A stunning building housing one of the finest collections of modern art in the world *(page 46)*

Millesgården • The home and studio of artist Carl Milles is itself a work of art *(page 64)*

Kungliga Slottet • The Changing of the Guard at the Royal Palace should not be missed *(page 30)*

A PERFECT DAY

9.00am **Breakfast**

Take advantage of the large spread of cooked meats, cheese, herring and smoked salmon that most hotels supply as a buffet breakfast.

12 noon **Retail therapy**

Pay a visit to one of Scandinavia's finest department stores, Nordiska Kompaniet (NK) and you will soon understand why Sweden has such a high reputation for design.

11.30am **Garden delight**

Head for Kungsträdgården, the former aristocratic gardens, to enjoy open-air concerts and street performance in summer and ice skating in winter.

1.30pm **Lunch**

At the northern end of Kungsträdgården is Victoria, a popular restaurant with outside tables facing on to the square where you can enjoy a plate of traditional Swedish meatballs.

10.00am **Gamla Stan gambol**

Walk over to Stockholm's Old Town to soak up the historic atmosphere and architecture and meander along the alleyways, including Mårten Trotzigs Gränd, the city's narrowest street. Browse in the shops on Västerlånggatan, then treat yourself to a coffee or an ice cream in Stortorget.

IN STOCKHOLM

5.30pm Cocktail hour

Enjoy a cocktail, or perhaps a glass of aquavit, at Josefina. If it's a sunny day be sure to find a seat outside on one of the sofas to do full justice to the waterfront views.

2.30pm Animal magic

Back at the waterfront, take the short boat trip to Djurgården, remembering to admire the grand façades of Strandvägen to your left en route, and reach Skansen in time to watch the brown bears being fed in the zoo area and perhaps watching crafts such as glass-blowing or pottery, depending on the calendar.

7.00pm Culture

Take a boat back to the city centre and enjoy either an operatic or ballet performance at Stockholm's historic Opera House (Operan).

9.00pm Musical chairs

Keeping with the operatic theme, have dinner at Operakällaren (book ahead) as much for the beautiful dining room as for the food. Or, for a slightly cheaper, less formal alternative, opt for the adjacent Café Opera, with its lovely Art Deco interior.

10.30pm Nightcap

Head north to Norrmalm, the main nightlife area of the city, for a shot or two of one of the 70 vodkas on offer at the Naglo Vodkabar. If you have more energy and fancy partying the night away, move on to nearby Spy Bar.

CONTENTS

14

30

64

82

98

73

INTRODUCTION

Stockholm, the capital of Sweden, well deserves the honour of being considered one of the most beautiful cities in the world. Dramatically situated at a point where the Baltic Sea and the waters of Lake Mälaren collide and fight for supremacy, the city has been splendidly endowed by nature. In fact, only the city centre to the north is situated on the mainland, with the rest of it spread gracefully, if unevenly, over 14 islands that are connected by no fewer than 40 bridges. This impressive scenario inspired the Swedish novelist Selma Lagerlöf to describe Stockholm as 'the city that floats on water'. Natural beauty, though, is just one part of the city's charm. Stockholm also has a glittering array of monuments, museums, restaurants and other fascinating attractions that will keep visitors thoroughly absorbed throughout their stay, whatever its length.

The Making of a Capital

Stockholm essentially owes its existence to its natural waterways, although we have the forward-thinking 13th-century regent Birger Jarl to thank for the sweeping city-on-water panorama that greets visitors to Stockholm today. Jarl (whose gold tomb statue is attached to the side of the Stadshuset – City Hall) ordered the fortification of a settlement between the Baltic Sea and Lake Mälaren in the 13th century, turning Stockholm into a major re-loading port for trading vessels plying northern Europe. With the Vikings long departed, and continental Europe entering a period of economic growth, this strategically placed settlement grew within a hundred years to become Sweden's largest.

Stockholm's City Hall

It's no wonder settlers were drawn to Stockholm. Various early conquerors left their mark in terms of magnificent pieces of architecture – notable among them were Gustav Vasa who instigated the building of the Tre Kronor (Three Crowns) castle, a landmark later transformed into a Renaissance palace; and Nicodemus Tessin the Elder, who as the city's first appointed architect was behind the new royal palace, the classical royal palace of Drottningholm and the beautiful and elegant Riddarhuset (House of Nobility). Nevertheless, it is Stockholm's extraordinary setting, scattered as it is across a series of sheltered water-filled bays and islands, that truly captures the imagination.

Stockholm has at various points been a significant cultural centre and key trading hub. Steam trains and freight trains, merchants and nobility have all passed through this city, leaving their mark in one way or another. In the drive

Celebrating New Year in Stockholm

for renewal following World War II, Stockholm endured its fair share of 1960s and 70s concrete blocks, mercifully curtailed in the mid-1970s. Thankfully, the city's shape and character, its classic buildings and medieval atmosphere remains largely intact. Today, the city is not only the seat of the national parliament (Riksdagshuset), the royal palace

Three Crowns

Gustav Vasa, who conquered the city from the Danes in 1523, built the original Tre Kronor (Three Crowns) castle. Adopted as the symbol of Stockholm, the Three Crowns are seen most dramatically at the very top of the Stadshuset (City Hall) tower.

(Kungliga slottet) and many other places of historical interest, but is also the country's financial and business hub. Even though Sweden is the fifth largest country in Europe after Russia, Ukraine, Spain and France, over one-sixth of the total population of Sweden calls the Stockholm area home.

The City that Floats on Water

Stockholm is a beguiling city – just when you think you know her, her mood changes once again. The melange of islands, districts and green zones comprising Sweden's 4,900 sq km (1,892 sq miles) create the illusion of a series of miniature and only distantly-related cities each with its own identity and charm.

Take the Old Town of Gamla Stan. It was on this island of antiquity at the heart of the city, around 1252, that Stockholm was born. A stroll along its meandering cloistered cobbled lanes flanked by perfectly preserved 15th- and 16th-century houses is to take a trip back to medieval times. In stark contrast, Norrmalm, the northern sector of town and location of Sergels Torg, with its glass and steel skyscrapers, malls, underpasses and roundabouts, has both feet planted firmly in the late 20th century. Blending into Norrmalm, to the east, is Östermalm, an up-market neighbourhood characterised by stately apartment buildings and home to many of the city's foreign embassies. Kungsholmen, the island just west of the city centre, hosts the municipal administration and is graced by the strikingly handsome Stadshuset rising from the shore of Lake Mälaren. Södermalm, the huge, hilly southern island that peers over the city showcases Stockholm's bohemian side – its lofty location and numerous artists' studios lending the island an atmosphere reminiscent of Montmartre. Here you'll find charming clusters of old wooden cottages hidden behind some of the city's trendiest galleries, boutiques and clubs.

The Cultural Scene

Culturally, Stockholm thrives as never before, especially in the performing arts, which receive large government subsidies. The public purse supports the internationally acclaimed 200-year-old Royal Opera (Operan), as well as the excellent Royal Dramatic Theatre (Kungliga Dramatiska Teatern). The

Underground Art

The Stockholm subway (tunnelbana, or T-bana), which evolved from an underground/overground tram system built in 1933, is one of the world's longest subway systems. Just over 39 miles (63km) of its total length of 62 miles (110km), are actually underground, as are around half of its 100 stations. But its most famous claim to fame is that it is considered to be the longest art gallery in the world. From its inception the tunnelbana doubled as a venue for displaying the work of the city's most creative artists, and millions of kroner are set aside annually to help maintain the tradition, which has so far showcased approximately 140 artists. As a result locals and tourists alike are treated to a succession of inventive paintings, murals, sculptures and mosaic works of art as they go about their daily commute.

city also boasts over 70 museums, more than enough to feed your cultural curiousity over any length stay. At one time nightlife was almost non-existent in Stockholm, but an explosion of nightclubs, trendy bars, contemporary restaurants and clubs has boosted the after-dark options considerably.

This is an affluent city. Stockholmers live and dress well, and in the shops you'll find plenty of the clean, no-nonsense designer goods that have put Swedish design

The T-bana subway is also the world's longest art gallery

on the international map, as well as some superb crystal from the glassworks district of Småland in the southeast of the country.

Once a relatively homogenous society, recent waves of immigration have brought a certain cultural diversity to the city. This is reflected in the widening in scope of restaurant menus, with French, Italian and a raft of ethnic cuisines taking their place alongside the traditional Swedish options. While eating out in Stockholm may not be cheap, you are generally guaranteed an eating experience unlike any you've had before.

Despite cultural innovations, many of the old Swedish traditions – such as the festivities on Midsummer Eve – remain an important part of Stockholm life. And while Stockholmers love a good meal, a night at the opera, and dancing till late at stylish nightclubs, even the most sophisticated city-dwellers are happiest when they can retreat into nature to walk, cycle or swim naked in tranquility.

Waving the flag on
National Day

Swedes and Stockholmers

What about the Swedes themselves? One could generalise by saying that they are a very pragmatic, orderly and reserved people with a strong sense of social consciousness and a progressive attitude to social welfare. Some of their more innovative laws are revered the world over. The Swedes also remain close to nature. In summer families generally retreat to a modest stuga, or summer house, often by a lake or surrounded by rustic woodland, for a taste of the simpler life. Between July and September, armies of berry-pickers and mushroom-hunters invade the forests.

As a summer city, Stockholm – and especially its lovely environs – is hard to beat. There is music and dancing in the city parks, concerts at the Royal Palace, and recital music drifts from many of the museums and churches. And, at this time, the city's graceful silhouette is bathed in the eerily beautiful midsummer light.

Stockholm is well worth visiting at other times of the year, too. There are some who admire it most in its autumn glory, or in the first flush of spring. And few could deny the enchanting beauty of the city in the dead of winter, when snow makes picture-postcard scenery from fairytale buildings, lanes and tiny squares; and the bays, channels and canals freeze over, allowing Stockholmers to walk, ski and skate over the waterways and inlets of the sea. It is fair to say that the spectacular seasonal transformations are just as much a key to discovering Stockholm as is the architectural juncture of old and new.

A BRIEF HISTORY

Archaeologists have established that Swedish history began somewhere around 12,000BC, when the miles-thick blanket of ice covering the whole continent began to melt. In the subsequent millennia, nomadic tribes of hunters and fishermen followed the receding ice cap northwards to the area that is now Sweden. In about 3000BC the inhabitants of the area were cultivating the land, raising livestock and living together in communities. Magnificent Bronze Age artefacts, including weapons and ornaments, indicate an early period of prosperity. Mysterious rock carvings of animals and people also survive from the prehistoric period.

By the time that Swedes are mentioned for the first instance in recorded history, however, conditions had altered substantially. This was in AD98, in Germania, where Roman historian Tacitus described the Sviones, or Svear tribe, as fierce warriors with mighty fleets of ships. They were based around Lake Mälaren, gradually rose to a position of dominance over neighbouring tribes, and by their seafaring exploits heralded the beginning of the Viking Age (AD800–1050).

Viking rune stone

The Vikings

The Vikings are best remembered for their ferocious raids on richer countries. They simply helped themselves to what they wanted, rather than eke out an existence in their harsh homeland. Some of the battles and exploits of this time are recorded on the thousands of rune stones to be found in Sweden.

However, the popular image of Vikings as the villains in history is being revised. Modern scholarship has revealed them to be remarkable poets and artists, explorers and settlers, who made many positive contributions to the territories they occupied. In their famous long ships, manned by as many as 50 oarsmen, these extraordinary seamen pushed west to Great Britain, taking large areas of France, and finally reaching North America. Those who travelled east established control over Novgorod and Kiev, and went on as far as Constantinople. The Vikings' navigational skills also equipped them for trading expeditions, and they became merchants as well as marauders.

History in the Field

Sweden's elongated landscape – stretching about a thousand miles from north to south – can be compared to a vast open-air museum.

Foremost are the Viking rune stones scattered throughout the country. These strange memorials record history and perpetuate myths. The hieroglyphics inscribed on their surfaces recount the everyday and heroic moments of the Viking warriors for whom the rune stones were raised. A fine selection is displayed in Stockholm's Historiska Museet (see page 60). Other features of the landscape dating from far-off times include cromlechs (stone burial enclosures), fabulous rock carvings of boats, animals and people, and Viking burial mounds.

Best of all are Sweden's lovely medieval country churches. Filled with well-preserved naive wood sculptures, stained-glass windows, altar paintings, and murals, they form an integral part of the countryside.

Early Christianity

Throughout the Viking period, Christian missionaries, mostly English and German monks, were active in Sweden. The first Christian church was founded in about AD830 in Birka by Ansgar, a monk from Picardy.

Christianising Sweden was an uphill battle, to say the least, and there were sporadic lapses into paganism as late as the 12th century. In Uppsala, for instance, yearly sacrificial feasts were held in honour of the Norse gods. By

Statue of Birger Jarl in Stockholm

the 13th century, however, the Church had become a dominant force in the country. The first archbishop, with a diocese in Uppsala, was appointed in 1164, and many churches were built during this period.

During the 13th century, a time of strife and contending factions, one important figure to emerge was Birger Jarl. Brother-in-law to the king, Jarl promoted the idea of a strong central government and also encouraged trade with other nations. When the king died, Birger Jarl had his own son elected heir to the throne. He is also credited with founding Stockholm, in about 1252, as a fort to protect against pirates.

The outstanding personality of the following century was St Birgitta, a religious mystic. Born in 1303, this remarkable woman was a prominent court figure, wife of a nobleman and mother of eight children. She founded a monastic order and church in the town of Vadstena in central Sweden, and her book, *Revelations* – translated into Latin and widely read in the Christian world – is considered a masterpiece of medieval literature. St Birgitta died in Rome, but her remains were brought back to Vadstena and buried in the church there.

The Kalmar Union

The so-called Kalmar Union was formed in 1397 to counteract the rapidly increasing power of the German Hanseatic League. It united Sweden, Denmark and Norway under a single ruler, the very able Queen Margareta of Denmark, making it Europe's largest kingdom.

Medieval Stockholm

The Swedes came to resent the dominance of the Danes and many were opposed to the union. In the 1430s they were led in a popular rebellion by the great Swedish hero Engelbrekt, who also assembled the first Swedish parliament in 1435. This Riksdag, which included representatives of the four estates – nobles, clergy, burghers and peasants – elected Engelbrekt regent of Sweden. Soon afterwards he was murdered and the unpopular union limped along until 1520. In that year the Scandinavian monarch, Christian II of Denmark, ruthlessly executed scores of Swedish noblemen, opponents who had been accused of heresy. However, instead of eliminating revolt, the 'Stockholm Bloodbath' unleashed a popular reaction that led to the disintegration of the despised Kalmar Union.

One of the noblemen who escaped death, Gustav Vasa, called on the peasants of the province of Dalarna to rebel against the Danish tyrant. With a ragtag army supported by foreign mercenaries, he succeeded in routing the Danes. He was crowned king in 1523 at the age of 27, and his dynamic reign dominated the 16th century.

Gustav Vasa was a strong-willed leader who reshaped the nation, earning himself the sobriquet 'Father of His Country'. He reorganised the state administration and stabilised its finances by, among other methods, confiscating all of the Church's considerable property holdings. After he died in 1560, three of his sons ruled Sweden in turn, and the Vasa dynasty survived for almost 150 years.

Sweden as a World Power

Foremost among the Vasa kings was Gustavus Adolphus, crowned Gustav II Adolf in 1611 aged 17. He promoted trade and industry and extended the borders of Sweden by conquests in Russia and Poland. Under his leadership Sweden became, for a time, the greatest power in 17th-century Europe. In 1632, Gustav II Adolf was killed in a battle at Lutzen defending the Protestant cause in the Thirty Years' War in Germany.

Gustav II Adolf

As his daughter Kristina was only six when Gustavus Adolphus died, the Count Axel Oxenstierna served as regent. Kristina was crowned in 1644. Very gifted but eccentric, she hated women and only socialised with men. Although making her court a brilliant salon, inviting to her capital famous European intellectuals such as the French philosopher Descartes, she was known to swear like a sailor. Ten years later, however, the queen startled the nation by abdicating; she converted to Catholicism and settled in Rome. She died in 1689 and is buried in St Peter's Cathedral there.

During the 17th century, Sweden, which had previously annexed Estonia, gained additional ground in the Baltic and along the German coasts and extended its borders into parts of Denmark and Norway. Sweden also established its first colony in America, in what is now Delaware, which was later captured by Britain. Sweden's final moments as a great power occurred under Karl (Charles) XII, who became monarch of the realm in 1697 at the age of 15. He is one of the most celebrated and controversial figures in the history of Sweden. Encouraged by a series of brilliant victories on the battlefield, the young king led his army deep into the interior of

Karl XII's army retreats

Russia in 1708–9, where he met with a disastrous defeat at Poltava in the Ukraine in the latter year.

After an extended exile in Turkey, Karl XII took up arms once more and was killed in Norway in 1718. His death marked the end of Sweden's Baltic Empire. Only Finland and part of Pomerania remained, and decades of unremitting warfare had left the country weak and in debt.

The Golden Age

The following years of peace were a golden age of culture and science. During this period, Carolus Linnaeus laid the foundations for modern botanical science by classifying the flora of the world, and Anders Celsius, the physicist and astronomer, developed the centigrade thermometer using a scale of 100 degrees between the freezing and boiling points of water.

Culture flourished during the reign of Gustav III (1771–92). The king, an ardent supporter of music, literature and art, founded the Royal Opera and the Swedish Academy (the Academy awards the Nobel Prize for Literature) to counter French influence and encourage the Swedish language. He also gave the nation what is known as the elegant 'Gustavian' style, the local version of Louis XVI style.

However, Gustav III was mortally wounded in an assassination attempt at a masked ball in the Stockholm Opera House, and Sweden was subsequently drawn into the Napoleonic Wars. In 1809 Finland, after having been a part of Sweden for 600 years, was possessed by Russia under an agreement between Czar Alexander I and Napoleon. In 1818 the Bernadotte dynasty was 'imported' from France and a field marshal under Napoleon, Jean Baptiste Bernadotte, was elected to the Swedish throne (as Karl XIV Johan), in the hope of obtaining French assistance in recovering Finland. In the event, Sweden participated in a final offensive to defeat Napoleon, with whom Denmark was allied. One of the results was

Setting off for the New World

Denmark's 1814 cession of Norway, which remained attached to Sweden until 1905.

An agricultural crisis hit Sweden towards the end of the 19th century. Hard times caused hundreds of thousands of Swedes to emigrate to America in the 1880s.

The 20th Century

The 20th century saw Sweden shifting rapidly from a farming economy to an industrial one. More and more people moved from rural areas to towns and cities. The emigration to America also continued, so that by 1930 about a million Swedes, one out of five, had settled in the New World.

At the same time, the power of the trade unions and their ally, the Social Democratic Party, founded in 1889, was increasing. Hjalmar Branting, the great socialist leader, became Prime Minister in 1920, setting the stage for vast social reforms that were to make Sweden the world's leading welfare state. Swedes may pay one of the highest rates of tax in the world to support cradle-to-grave security, but most of them feel that they get a lot in return for their money. This includes housing subsidies, maternity and paternity leave, child allowances, free hospital care, pensions and a host of other benefits – not to mention the right to five weeks paid leave annually. These and other social measures in operation, however, fall far short of classic socialism, and the bulk of Swedish industry is still controlled by private interests. The success of their exploitation of the few natural resources – namely iron ore and timber – has not only made the welfare state possible, but has also allowed for one of the world's highest standards of living.

Swedish technical genius has played a significant role in building an affluent society as well. Many of Sweden's international companies have been developed on the basis of Swedish inventions such as dynamite (invented by Alfred Nobel; *see page 32*), the modern calculator (Wilgodt T. Odhner), and the important three-phase alternating electrical current system (Jonas Wenström).

Sweden remains a constitutional monarchy with the king as head of state, but actual power rests solely with parliament, which since 1971 has consisted of a single chamber with 350 members. The Social Democrats have been the dominant faction in modern Swedish politics. Nonetheless, the country has mostly been governed by consensus, with political decisions reached by discreet compromise. All of the nation's political parties have supported the broad outlines of the welfare state.

The Swedish Monarchy

The traditions of monarchy in Sweden date back more than a millennium, and it was during the reign of Gustav Vasa, who was elected king on 6 June 1523, that the right of succession to inherit the Swedish crown was established.

The current dynasty came about because the then monarch, Karl XIII, was childless. Jean-Baptiste Bernadotte, a general and marshal of the French Empire under Napoleon, was well respected by the Swedes when he showed much consideration of Scandinavian prisoners while he served as governor of the Hanseatic cities between 1807–08. Karl XIII recognised his talents and designated him as his heir apparent. Bernadotte came to the throne in 1818 as King Karl XIV Johan. The present monarch, King Carl XVI Gustaf, is the seventh in the Bernadotte dynasty and has reigned since 1973. He will be succeeded by his daughter, Crown Princess Victoria.

From the 19th century all the way through to the 21st century, Sweden can look back on a time of almost uninterrupted peace and stability. It fought its last war in 1814, and adopted a strict policy of neutrality that kept it out of both world wars. Notwithstanding their capacity for neutrality and compromise, Swedes make a concerted effort to avoid isolationist policies.

Modern Times

The country has supported the United Nations since its inception, but despite its peaceful reputation political assassinations occurred on 28 February 1986, when the Prime Minister Olof Palme was shot on a street, and again on 10 September 2003, when Anna Lindh, the foreign minister, was stabbed to death in the Nordiska Kompaniet shopping mall.

Sweden joined the European Union in 1995, and to reflect that new European status Stockholm was selected as the Culture Capital of Europe for 1998. However, it decided not to join the European single currency at its inception in 1999, as the government considered that the economic conditions were not favourable and popular support wasn't agreeable either. In 2003, the euro was rejected by popular referendum.

Head of state, King Carl XVI Gustaf, and Queen Silvia

In 2006, a centre-right alliance headed by the Moderate Party under the leadership of Fredrik Reinfeldt won the election with a narrow majority, thus ending 12 years of Social Democrat rule. In 2010 the Alliance failed to gain a majority but is still in power as a minority government.

Historical Landmarks

c.1252 Stockholm founded, probably by Birger Jarl.

1397 Kalmar Union links the Nordic countries.

1520 Swedish noblemen executed in the 'Stockholm Bloodbath'.

1523 Gustav Vasa crowned king of Sweden after defeating the Danes.

1527 Parliament confiscates Church property during the Reformation.

1611 Gustav II Adolf comes to power.

1618 The Thirty Years' War starts in Germany.

1644 Gustav's daughter Kristina crowned.

1654 Kristina abdicates, converts to Catholicism and moves to Rome.

1697 Tre Kronor Castle destroyed by fire; Karl XII, aged 15, is crowned.

1719 Constitution transfers power from the king to parliament.

1772 King Gustav III reclaims absolute power.

1786 Swedish Academy founded.

1809 Sweden loses Finland; Gustav IV Adolf abdicates.

1814 Sweden gains Norway in peace with Denmark.

1818 Karl XIV Johan crowned king of Sweden and Norway.

1850 Sweden's population reaches 3.5 million (93,000 in Stockholm).

1869 Emigration to North America increases due to crop failures.

1876 L.M. Eriksson starts the manufacture of telephones.

1895 Alfred Nobel establishes the Nobel Prize.

1905 Parliament dissolves the union with Norway.

1939 Sweden's coalition government declares neutrality in World War II.

1950 Stockholm's first underground railway is inaugurated.

1955 Obligatory national health insurance established.

1974 The monarch loses all political powers.

1986 Prime Minister Olof Palme is murdered in Stockholm.

1995 Sweden joins the European Union after a referendum.

2000 Church separates from the state after 400 years.

2003 Foreign Minister Anna Lindh murdered in Stockholm.

2006 Centre-right alliance headed by the Moderate Party wins election.

2010 The Sweden Democrats, a far right party, gain parliamentary seats for the first time.

WHERE TO GO

At first glance, visitors to Stockholm may feel that the unusual, if not unique, geographical combination of islands and water might make the city difficult to navigate and somewhat confusing. However, this is most certainly not the case. In fact, on arrival, most people will find themselves in Norrmalm, the more modern – and somewhat less attractive – part of the city centre, where a combination of proximity to major hotels, shops and sights of interest reached by an array of efficient public transport – buses, subway, trams and ferries – makes getting around easier than one might think. Visitors may find it helpful to acquaint themselves with Stockholm by taking a boat tour of the city (see page 122), although wandering on foot remains the best way to explore.

> **Viewing the city**
>
> For a visual introduction to Stockholm, catch a number 69 bus from Sweden House (the tourist office) to the 155m (508ft) tall TV tower, Kaknästornet (June–Aug daily 9am–10pm; Sept–May Mon–Sat 10am–9pm, Sun 10am–6pm; charge). Its observation platform offers stunning views.

GAMLA STAN

The high island rising between the waters of the Baltic Sea and Lake Mälaren is known as **Gamla Stan** – the Old Town. However, in the 13th century it was called Stadsholmen and its naturally defensive position (between two narrow channels of water connecting the sea and lake) made it an ideal place for Birger Jarl to construct a fortress and begin the foundations of the city. Thus Stockholm's history is concentrated in Gamla

Gamla Stan and Riddarholm Church

Stan and its cobbled lanes, winding alleys, mansions, palaces and soaring spires.

Exploring Gamla Stan is a must for every visitor to Stockholm. Starting from Gustav Adolfs Torg, cross over the gracefully arched bridge of Norrbro. The massive façade of the Royal Palace beckons, but before going there spend a few moments on the first island – one of the four comprising Gamla Stan. On your right will be the **Riksdagshuset**, the House of Parliament (guided tours Oct–mid-June Sat–Sun 1.30pm, mid-June–Aug Mon–Fri noon, 1pm, 2pm, 3pm; www.riksdagen.se; free). To the left, steps lead down to a small park, **Stromparterren**, home to the Museum of Medieval Stockholm and a café along the banks of the Norrström channel. This is where the waters of the Baltic and Lake Mälaren meet. You may see fishermen on the bankside or standing in the water. The Stockholm authorities actually encourage this and no permit is required. There is even a set of weighing scales in the park to check if a trophy fish has been caught.

Kungliga Slottet

Now cross the next bridge over the narrow Stallkanalen waterway, and head up the hill to the **Kungliga Slottet** (Royal Palace; mid-May–mid-Sept daily 10am–5pm, mid-Sept–mid-May Tue–Sun noon–4pm; charge; www.royalcourt.se). Built on the site of the original Tre Kronor (Three Crowns) castle, it was commissioned by King Karl XI, and the architect Nicodemus Tessin the Younger began work on it in 1692. However, a combination of a fire in 1697 and a subsequent poor economy delayed continuation until 1728. It wasn't until 1754 that King Adolf Fredrik was able to move in, ending the royal family's 57 years of residence in the Wrangelska palace on the island of Riddarholmen. It is still the official residence of His Majesty the King, and until the present monarch, Carl XVI Gustaf, decided to reside at Drottningholm, it was known as one of the biggest palaces in the world (over 600 rooms) still to be inhabited by royalty.

Kungliga Slottet is remarkably accessible to the public, although parts, or all, may be closed for affairs of state. Anyone can walk through the inner courtyard, and the main parts of the building are open to visitors. Be sure not to miss the beautifully preserved rococo interior of the **Royal Chapel** and Queen Kristina's silver throne in the Hall of State. Among other palace highlights are the **Royal Apartments** and **Galleries** with magnificent baroque interiors, containing priceless 17th-century Gobelin tapestries, paintings, china, jewellery and furniture collected over the centuries by kings and queens. The royal jewels are displayed in the **Treasury** (Skattkammaren) and include the king's crown, first used for Erik XIV's coronation in 1561, and the queen's crown, designed in 1751 for Queen Lovisa Ulrika, which is spectacularly studded with

Inside Kungliga Slottet

almost 700 diamonds. In addition to housing the Treasury, the **Palace Museum** in the cellar has artefacts from the Middle Ages, and the Museum of Antiquities exhibits classical sculpture brought from Italy by King Gustav III during the 1780s.

Also located in the complex is **Livrustkammaren** (Royal Armoury; July–Aug daily 10am–6pm, Sept–Apr Tue–Sun 11am–5pm, Thur until 8pm, May–June daily 11am–5pm; charge; www.livrustkammaren.se), a fascinating collection of the weapons and costumes of Swedish kings and queens. Some of the more esoteric exhibits you'll see include a horse ridden by Gustavus Adolphus when he fell in the Battle of Lützen in 1632, cleverly preserved by a taxidermist; the uniform that Charles XII was wearing when he was fatally wounded in the trenches while besieging Fredrikshald, Norway, in 1718; and the costume Gustav III wore when he was murdered at the Opera Ball, together with the assassin's gun and mask.

No visit to the Kungliga Slottet is complete without taking time to witness the ritual **Changing of the Guard** in the outer courtyard (www.forsvarsmakten.se; Apr–Aug Mon–Sat 11.45am, Sun and hols 12.45pm, Sept–Oct Wed, Sat–Sun same times, Nov–Mar Wed, Sat and Sun 12.09pm). The approximately 4,000 conscripts who serve as guards each year come from about 40 army, navy and air force units from all over Sweden. And this is just not an honorary force, but also an important part of military readiness in Stockholm. That said, Sweden, once a mighty military power in northern Europe, has not been involved in a war since the early 19th century. The

Changing of the Guard

Inside Storkyrkan

event is certainly ceremonial, although it is not as formal an occasion as it is elsewhere. In fact, on one occasion, two guards hilariously marched away from the troop instead of with it.

Storkyrkan and Stortorget

Just south of the palace on Slottsbacken, and diagonally across from the south façade, is **Storkyrkan** (Great Church). It is the city's oldest church, dating from the 13th century, and it has been the coronation site of most of Sweden's kings. Storkyrkan's dull baroque exterior gives no hint of the beauty of its late-Gothic interior. Of note is the sculptural depiction of St George and the Dragon, which symbolises Sweden's struggles to break free of Denmark. The sculpture was executed by Bernt Notke, a woodcarver from the German city of Lübeck, in the 15th century.

Just a few steps from the church, in **Stortorget** (Great Square), a murderous event known as the 'Stockholm Blood

Bath' took place in 1520. King Christian II of Denmark ordered the beheading of some 80 Swedish noblemen here, and their heads were piled pyramid-style in the middle of the square. Among the fine old houses on Stortorget is the **Börsen** (Stock Exchange), a handsome building dating from 1776. The Swedish Academy meets here to elect the Nobel Prize winners in literature. The building is also home to the **Nobelmuseet** (The Nobel Museum; mid-May–mid-Sept daily 10am–6pm, Tue until 8pm, mid-Sept–mid-May Tue 11am–8pm, Wed–Sun 11am–5pm; charge; www.nobel-

The Pacifist Who Invented Dynamite

Alfred Nobel (1833–96) became a first-rate chemist while still in his teens. Inventor, engineer and industrialist, he held a total of 355 patents during his lifetime. A pacifist at heart, he invented dynamite, which proved a boon to modern warfare. Nobel also patented blasting gelatin, and invented smokeless gunpowder. These products formed the basis of his industrial empire, which spread across five continents.

Alfred Nobel established the celebrated Nobel prizes in his will, drawn up a year before his death. These were for physics and chemistry (awarded by the Swedish Academy of Sciences), for physiological or medical works (awarded by the Karolinska Institute in Stockholm), for literature (awarded by the Academy in Stockholm), and for champions of peace (awarded by a committee of five elected by the Norwegian Storting). They were to go to those who 'shall have conferred the greatest benefit on mankind' with the stipulation that 'no consideration whatever shall be given to the nationality of the candidates'. His entire fortune was dedicated to this purpose.

First awarded in 1901, the prizes for the first four categories have been given at the Nobel Dinner held at Stockholm's Stadshuset (City Hall) on 10 December each year. Nobel directed that the Peace prize be awarded in Oslo, which at his death, and until 1905, was part of Sweden.

museum.se), which uses cutting-edge design and technology, including 40 fascinating short films, to document the history and the world of the Nobel Prize – specifically Alfred Nobel himself and the more than 700 laureates.

Exploring the Old Town

Once you've seen the principal attractions, the best way to get the feel of the Old Town is to wander its maze of medieval stone streets at

Stockholm's narrowest street, Mårten Trotzigs Gränd

will. There's something to experience at every turn – antiques shops housed in fine 15th- and 16th-century buildings, former merchant palaces, gabled houses decorated with ornate portals and delightful alleyways with names like Gåsgränd (Goose Lane) and Skeppar Karls Gränd (Skipper Karl's Lane). You'll also come across art shops, galleries and smart boutiques selling clothes, handcrafted jewellery and ceramics and plenty of cosy cafés serving decent coffee and *kanelbulle* (cinnamon rolls).

Two streets emanate southwards from either side of the Kungliga Slottet, Västerlanggatan to the west and Österlänggatan to the east, finally curving together at the small square of Järntorget (the Iron Market Square). These two streets adjoined the original city walls, and the area inside them plus the palace actually constitute the original Old Town.

Västerlånggatan (pedestrian-only) and Österlånggatan are interesting and contrasting streets in their own right.

The former, lined along its entirety with tourist shops of every description, bars and restaurants, is much more popular and is usually extremely crowded. At Tyska Brinken make a short detour to the left and go to **Tyska Kyrkan** (German Church). It boasts a fine baroque exterior and an opulent interior dating from the mid-17th century. Near the end, also on the left, is **Mårten Trotzigs Gränd**, the narrowest street in Stockholm. This steep, lamp-lit, stone stairway is scarcely more than a yard wide and takes you on to Prästgatan.

Past Järntorget, swing left into **Österlånggatan**, another long, winding street. Despite being dotted with art galleries, craftsmen's shops and some fine restaurants, it is noticeably more tranquil. At number 51 is **Den Gyldene Freden** (The Golden Peace), the most famous restaurant in the Old Town. Its name comes from the Peace of Nystad of 1721, which marked the end of Charles XII's wars. The historic brick cellar rooms are associated with the 18th-century troubadour Carl Michaël Bellman, who dropped by here from time to time. Walking north, you will pass by another statue of St George and the Dragon and a number of small boutiques to tempt your wallet.

That sinking feeling

Many beautiful and grand old buildings can be found along Skeppsbron, but these were built on land reclaimed from the archipelago and if you look closely, particularly at those nearest to Slussen, you will notice that they have been affected by subsidence.

The areas to either side of Österlånggatan and Västerlånggatan are reclaimed land. To the east of the former, narrow picturesque lanes with arched entrances and small streets lead to the long, wide, waterfront thoroughfare of **Skeppsbron**. The structures here are of a grand style and the quayside is lined with a vast array of vessels. These range from ferry-boats to restaurant boats, a Viking ship for harbour cruises and the most magnificent cruise ships you are likely to see.

The larger, western side of Gamla Stan is bisected by the rather busy Stora Nygatan, making it somewhat less attractive. At its northern end is a square called **Riddarhustorget**. This was where the assassin of Gustav III was brutally flogged before being beheaded. On the north side of the square is the classic 17th-century **Riddarhuset** (House of Nobility; all year Mon–Fri 11.30am–12.30pm; charge; www.riddarhuset.se). Arguably Stockholm's most beautiful building, its interior is distinguished by 2,325 coats of arms of noble Swedish families. The original architect, Vallée, a Frenchman, was tragically stabbed to death in a dispute over the building plans, but a German, a Dutchman and the original architect's son, Jean de la Vallée, finally completed the admirable red-brick and sandstone structure. To this day, members of these noble families can hire the hall for weddings or other such social occasions.

The impressive Riddarhuset

South of here, on the parallel street of Lilla Nygatan, is the **Postmuseum** (Tue–Sun 11am–4pm, Sept–Apr Wed until 7pm; charge; www.postmuseum.posten.se), which documents the history of the mail service in Sweden from 1636 to the present. The museum contains an excellent philatelic department – in fact, it is one of the largest stamp collections on public view in the world. Among the rarities is the first English stamp, cancelled on the day of issue, 6 May 1840.

Riddarholmen

Cross the nearby bridge, Riddarholmsbron, to arrive on the island of **Riddarholmen** (Isle of the Nobility). Here, you'll find a former Riksdag (Parliament) building, several palaces, and the copper-topped Birger Jarl's tower, erected by Gustav Vasa in the 16th century. At Riddarholmen quay you get a marvellous view of Lake Mälaren, the heights of Söder (southern Stockholm) and Stadshuset on Kungsholmen *(see page 41)*, which appears as though it is rising straight out of Lake Mälaren.

> ### Floating restaurant
>
> The *Mälardrottningen*, a shining white yacht moored to Riddarholmen, was once the plaything of American billionairess Barbara Hutton. Now a floating hotel and restaurant, it's a great spot for dining on a summer evening.

It is the elegantly intricate façade, with its distinctive cast-iron latticework spire, of the **Riddarholmskyrkan** ◄❼ (Riddarholm Church; mid-May–mid-Sept daily 10am–5pm; charge; www.royal court.se) that dominates this small island. Built in connection with a Franciscan monastery founded by King Magnus Ladulås in 1270, it was completed very early in the 14th century and has been the burial place of Swedish kings for some 500 years. The interior is a pleas-

ing mix of simplicity and re-
gality. The walls are covered
in the coats of arms of the
Knights of the Seraphim
Order. The floor contains
about 200 graves from different eras. The last regular
service was held here in
1807. These days it is only
used for memorial and burial services.

NORRMALM AND KUNGSHOLMEN

You will, undoubtedly, be
spending some time in the
New Stockholm, or Norr-
malm, the city's northern
sector. This is where the business, banking, shopping and
entertainment facilities are

A row of skyscrapers
dominates Norrmalm's skyline

concentrated, as well as the majority of larger hotels and the
railway and bus stations.

In the post-war renewal between the 1950s and the early
1970s, central Stockholm was almost entirely rebuilt and old
streets were replaced by office blocks and modern shopping
malls with restaurants, cinemas and boutiques.

Sergels Torg
Stockholm's equivalent of Trafalgar Square, or Times Square,
is found at the bi-level **Sergels Torg** (Sergel Square), which
has become the focal point of the modern city. Named after
Johan Tobias Sergel, an 18th-century court sculptor, it is the

The bright lights of Sergels Torg

centre of the city's shopping district with traffic circling around a huge glass obelisk that sits in the centre of a fountain, and an open-air pedestrian precinct on the lower level. The market stalls, protesters and street entertainers here attract many shoppers and curious onlookers.

The dominant building is the huge, glass-fronted **Kulturhuset** (Culture Centre; www.kulturhuset.se), where hundreds of people come daily to see art and handicraft exhibitions, watch films, listen to music, poetry and dramatic readings, or read the latest editions of newspapers from around the world at the World News Café. The **Stockholm Stadsteater** (Municipal Theatre), which stages modern and classical plays in Swedish, is also located here.

North of Sergels Torg

A short walk through the city's shopping centre, a mix of malls and shopping streets usually animated by the music of street performers, will take you to **Hötorget** (Haymarket Square), the northern end of the row of glass skyscrapers that starts at Sergels Torg. Hötorget's open-air market – selling fresh fruit, vegetables and flowers six days a week and operating as a flea market on Sunday – adds a touch of colour to the square. Also on Hötorget, you will find **Konserthuset** (Concert Hall; www.konserthuset.se), a neoclassical building distinguished by an unusual façade of Corinthian pillars and bronze portals. The Stockholm Philharmonic Orchestra performs here, but you can hear other kinds of music, from chamber music to pop melodies. In front of the building you will see Carl Milles' **Orpheus Fountain**, one of the late Swedish sculptor's finest works *(see page 64)*.

At the northern end of the shopping street of Drottninggatan you will find the interesting **Strindbergsmuseet**  (Strindberg Museum; Tue–Sat noon–4pm; charge; www. strindbergsmuseet.se). Here, the apartment in which Sweden's greatest playwright, August Strindberg, lived during the last years of his life has been reconstructed with authentic furnishings, including his original writing desk. Three adjoining rooms are devoted to his manuscripts, letters and the photos of actors and actresses who performed roles in his plays. Strindberg died in 1912.

Nordiska Kompaniet

Kungsträdgården and Environs

Leading east from Sergels Torg is **Hamngatan**, one of the main shopping streets. Its tenants include NK (short for Nordiska Kompaniet), Sweden's biggest department store, alongside Gallerian, a mall with many shops and restaurants. **Sverigehuset** (Sweden House) supplies information about Sweden. Inside, a regional tourist office provides maps and guides of Stockholm and surrounding areas, as well as a money exchange office and a souvenir shop. Tickets for the theatre, concerts and sports events can also be purchased here.

9 ➤ Next door is Stockholm's liveliest park, **Kungsträdgården** (Royal Gardens), stretching from Hamngatan down to the waters of Strömmen. Established as a royal pleasure garden in the 16th century for the exclusive use of the Swedish aristocracy and the court, Kungsträdgården has now become a favourite gathering place for locals and visitors especially during the summer months. Encircled by cafés and restaurants you will find a long, rectangular pond with fountains; an outdoor stage for rock, chamber music and choral concerts; botanical exhibits, statues and an ice-skating rink during winter.

Playtime in the park

At the foot of the Kungsträdgården is a small, attractive park, Karl XII's Torg. It is dominated by a statue of the king himself, Sweden's most celebrated historical figure. Behind this park the outline of the 17th-century church **Jakobs Kyrka** dominates. It is worth a moment here to look at the marvellous portals, particularly the one on the southern side, which dates from 1644.

Just west of here is **Gustav Adolfs Torg**, a large square with an equestrian statue of King Gustavus Adolphus, the Swedish hero of the Thirty Years' War. On the east side of the square you will see **Operan** (Royal Opera; www.operan.se), housed in a sombre baroque-style building from 1898. King Gustav III, a great patron of the arts, founded the opera in 1773. It was here (in the original opera house) that he was shot and killed some 20 years later at a masked ball. Incidentally, Verdi used this drama as the basis for his opera *The Masked Ball*. Swedes are proud of the Royal Opera's long and distinguished history. Some of the world's greatest singers got their start here, from Jenny Lind, the 19th-century 'Swedish Nightingale' who made a fabulously successful tour around the United States, to Jussi Björling and Birgit Nilsson. This remarkable institution has a breathtaking output of nearly 400 performances of opera and ballet each season.

On the southwest side of Gustav Adolfs Torg is **Arv-furstens Palats** (Prince's Palace), which in 1906 was taken over by the Swedish Foreign Office.

Kungsholmen

Just west of Norrmalm, Kungsholmen (King's Island) is a well-to-do area, but it retains a quiet, neighbourhood feel and, at just under 4 sq km (1½ sq miles), is very manageable. The opening of the boutique shopping centre, Vastermalmsgallerian, in 2000, was the catalyst for a blossoming café, bistro and bar scene and its numerous and attractive little restaurants offer an easy diversion from the bustle of the city. The view from its city hall tower is a must for visitors.

Cross Stadshusbron (City Hall Bridge) from Tegelbacken, just a short walk from Central Station, and on your left is Stockholm's majestic **Stadshuset** (City Hall; guided tours June–Aug daily half hourly 9.30am–4pm, tours may be cancelled due to a reception; tower: daily May–Sept 9.15am–4pm, until 5.15pm June–Aug; charge; www.stockholm.se/

City Hall

stadshuset). When W.B. Yeats came to Stockholm in 1923 to receive the Nobel Prize for Literature, he took a look at the new City Hall and exclaimed that 'no work comparable in method and achievement has been accomplished since the Italian cities felt the excitement of the Renaissance...'

Yeats was not alone in lavishing praise on Stockholm's City Hall. Designed by Ragnar Östberg, the building rises gracefully and dramatically from the shore of Lake Mälaren. Artists and craftsmen from all over Sweden contributed to its creation, and it has become a fitting symbol – almost an architectural hymn to the city. Stadshuset is worth several hours of your time, and even then you'll only get an inkling of what went into the construction of this remarkable building. The special hand-cut brick façades – made of over 8 million bricks; the imposing square tower capped by three golden crowns; the black granite reliefs, pillars and arches. All miraculously work together to form a unified and coherent whole, a monumental attempt to fuse the many different elements that make up Stockholm. It was inaugurated on Midsummer Day in 1923, the 400th anniversary of Gustav Vasa's coronation on the day he marched into town.

Join one of the guided tours through the handsome interior of City Hall. Highlights include the **Golden Hall**, covered with striking mosaics, the huge glass-domed **Blue Hall** (which is actually red) where the Nobel Prize banquets are held, and the **Prince's Gallery**, with murals executed by Prince Eugen.

The original idea was that all materials used in the construction and decoration were to be Swedish. However, the architect was faced with a problem when the French Government made a gift of the Tureholm tapestries, which were woven at Beauvais in France at the end of the 17th century. He resolved this by placing them in a rather small, round room. Today, this is where civil weddings are conducted and the happy couples have a choice of two ceremonies; one that lasts 3 minutes and the other all of 7 seconds.

In a terraced garden by the water lie Carl Eldh's sculptures of the dramatist August Strindberg, the poet Gustaf Fröding and the painter Ernst Josephson. Also here, on top of a 14m (46ft) high column, is Christian Eriksson's bronze statue of Engelbrekt, Sweden's great hero of the Middle Ages.

The Golden Hall

For a superb view of the Old Town and central Stockholm, if you have the energy, walk to the top of the 115m (350ft) tall City Hall Tower.

Extending west of Stadshuset is **Norr Mälarstrand**, a landscaped promenade that follows the water's edge all the way to the **Västerbron** (Western Bridge). This pleasant walk is often crowded with Stockholmers out for a casual stroll, with many parents pushing prams, and is especially popular on a sunny Sunday afternoon.

THE MUSEUM ISLANDS

Situated to the east of Gamla Stan, the 'museum islands' of Blasieholmen and Skeppsholmen are where you can steep yourself in Scandinavian art, architecture and design, as well as take in some pretty walks. Skeppsholmen was once a centre of naval architecture and a pleasant amble around it will reveal some key naval sights, such as the fully rigged *Af Chapman* schooner.

Now a peninsula between Norrmalm and Skeppsholmen, Blasieholmen is home to the Nationalmuseet (National Museum). The pretty Berzelli Park is situated to the northeast.

Blasieholmen

The island of Blasieholmen is home to a number of elegant palaces built during the 17th and 18th centuries. Two of the city's oldest palaces are situated at **Blasieholmstorg**. The palace at number 8 was built in the mid-17th century and later rebuilt in the style of an 18th-century French palace. It used to host foreign ambassadors and is now known as Utrikesministerhotellet (Foreign Ministry Hotel), home to the Musical Academy and Swedish Institute. Bååtska Palatset stands nearby at number 6. Dating from 1699, it was partly rebuilt in 1876 for the freemasons, who still have their lodge here. Southwest along Stallgatan is one of Scandinavia's most famous hotels, the impressive **Grand Hôtel**, which overlooks Strömkajen, the departure point for Stockholm's numerous sightseeing boats.

At the tip of Blasieholmen, along Sodra Blasieholmen, is the imposing façade of the **Nationalmuseum** (National Museum of Fine Arts; Tue 11am–8pm, Wed–Sun 11am–5pm; charge; www.nationalmuseum.se). One of the world's oldest museums, it was founded in 1792, when it occupied a wing of the Royal Palace and was known as the Royal Museum. It moved to its current home, a massively impressive Italian Renaissance-style building, in 1866.

The collection is impressive, and not only because of the size and scope of the paintings, sculptures, decorative arts, drawings and prints. Among the old masters collection you'll find Rembrandts, plus important works by El Greco, Rubens, Goya and Brueghel, and a choice selection of Chardin oils. Courbet, Cézanne, Gauguin, Renoir and Manet are represented here, as are important Swedish artists, including Carl Larsson, Anders Zorn and Bruno Liljefors (known for his vivid nature studies). Zorn's *Midsummer Dance* is a wonderful evocation of Midsummer's Eve in the province of Dalarna.

The National Museum

Other paintings to look for include François Boucher's *The Triumph of Venus*, considered his greatest work, and *The Lady and the Veil* by the Swedish painter Alexander Roslin (1718–93). In addition to these treats, there are thousands of prints, engravings and miniatures, more than 200 Russian icons, and a selection of handicrafts to appreciate.

Skeppsholmen

The narrow stretch of water between Blasieholmen and Skeppsholmen is surmounted by a small wrought-iron bridge, Skeppsholmsbron. From the bridge there are magnificent views across to Strandvägen. The sleek schooner moored off the island is the *Af Chapman*, over 100 years old and used as a youth hostel and café. There are three museums here worthy of investigation.

Museum of Modern Art

Crossing the small bridge, Skeppsholmbron, will bring you to the **Moderna Museet** (Tue 10am–8pm, Wed–Sun 10am–6pm; charge; www.modernamuseet.se). Housed in a stunning building designed by the prize-winning Spanish architect Rafael Moneo and opened in 1998 to celebrate Stockholm's role as the European City of Culture, and re-

Investigating an exhibit at the Moderna Museet

opened in 2004 after extensive renovation, the museum's large collection of 20th-century art includes works by Léger, Matisse, Braque, Modigliani, Klee and Rauschenberg, as well as by such notable Swedish artists as Isaac Grünewald and Bror Hjorth. The benefit of the museum's island location is best appreciated from its restaurant and café (with terrace), which afford wonderful waterside views thanks to generous floor-to-ceiling windows.

Swedish Museum of Architecture

The **Arkitekturmuseet** (opening times as Moderna Museet; charge; audioguide available; www.arkitekturmuseet. se) shares the entrance to the Moderna Museet. The collection guides visitors through 1,000 years of Scandinavian building, from the simplest wooden houses to state-of-the-art techniques and styles. There are models of architectural works worldwide, from 2000BC to the present day. The museum's archive contains 2 million drawings and sketches and 600,000 photographs, all available for visitors to peruse.

The Museum of Far Eastern Antiquities

The third museum reached by crossing Skeppsholmsbron is located at the northern tip of Skeppsholmen. **Östasiatiska Museet** (Tue 11am–8pm, Wed–Sun 11am–5pm; charge; www.ostasiatiska.se) is housed in a building dating from 1700, which was originally designed as a stable and quarters for Charles XII's bodyguards. The museum's enormous collection embraces art from Japan, Korea, India and China from the Stone Age to the 19th century. Its collection of ancient Chinese art, considered the best in the world outside of China, includes 1,800 objects given to the museum in 1974 by the late King Gustaf VI Adolf, a distinguished archaeologist and a respected authority on Chinese art.

The museum's stand-out exhibits are numerous and include ancient Stone Age pottery, a reconstructed Chinese grave furnished with urns and axe heads grouped around a skeleton, colourful ceramics dating from the Ming Dynasty (1368–1644), and a series of highly impressive 3,000-year-old bronze sacrificial vessels.

DJURGÅRDEN

It's easy to see why Stockholmers love Djurgården. This immense, largely unspoiled island of natural beauty used to be a royal hunting park, and is still controlled by the king to this day. In addition to miles of woodland trails and magnificent oaks, some of which go back to Viking times, it contains surprising statuary tucked away amid its greenery, outdoor coffee shops and restaurants, an amusement park and some of the city's principal museums. Djurgården is perfect for picnicking, jogging, horse riding, or just enjoying a quiet walk. One of the favourite promenades for strollers lies along a path that winds and dips but never strays too far from the shoreline.

Taking the ferry across the Djurgårdsbrunnsviken

Actually, Djurgården consists of two large tracts of land west of the city proper,

divided from each other by
the east/west axis of **Djurgårdsbrunnsviken**, a lovely
channel that merges with an
even lovelier canal. In winter,
when the water freezes over,
people ski or skate on the ice
here. To the visitor, this area
can be somewhat confusing,
as the northern part is shown
on maps and guides as

Ferry service

Waxholmsbolaget operates
a frequent daily ferry service
from Slussen to Allmänna
Gränd on Djurgården (via
Skeppsholmen in winter;
www.waxholmsbolaget.se).
You can also catch Strömma
ferry boats from Nybroplan
(June–mid-Sept).

Ladugårdsgärdet. Although the TV tower *(see page 27)*, Sjöhistoriska Museet (National Maritime Museum; *see page 61*) and
two other museums are found on this side, they don't attract
too many visitors. In fact, the vast majority of visitors to Stockholm will find themselves drawn to the western end of the island actually named Djurgården, to the south.

There is a variety of transport available here. Most fun,
is to take the number 7 tram from Norrmalmstorg – near
Sweden House – and from the same place there also is the
option of the number 47 bus. Incidentally, regular tram service was discontinued in 1967 when Sweden switched from
left- to right-hand driving, and this line was re-opened as a
charity operated museum line in 1991. Now there's even a
café tram. Look for the enormous coffee cup on its roof. An
even better alternative, given fine weather, is to go on foot
and return by one of the above suggestions. Start at Nybroplan and follow Strandvägen *(see page 60)* in the Östermalm section of town until you reach Djurgårdsbron, the
bridge to Djurgården.

Nordic Museum

After crossing the bridge, the huge multi-towered building
on your right is the home of the **Nordiska Museet** (Nordic

Museum; Djurgårdsvägen 6-16; Mon–Tue, Thur–Sat 10am–5pm, Wed 10am–8pm, Sun 11am–5pm; charge, free Wed 4–8pm; www.nordiskamuseet.se). Housed in one of the most impressive buildings in Stockholm, dating from 1907, this museum, illustrating life in Sweden from the 16th century to the present, is the brainchild of Artur Hazelius, also the creator of Skansen.

Entering the building, you are greeted by Carl Milles' enormous oak statue of Gustav Vasa, father of modern Sweden (*see page 19*). There is a lot to view here – more than 1 million objects, in fact. You'll find exhibits depicting the history of upper-class fashions, an interesting section on food and drink with table settings from different periods, and a costume gallery devoted to Swedish peasant dress from the beginning of the 19th century. There's also a feature on the nomadic Lapps and their reindeer and an exhibition concentrating on Nordic folk art that includes Swedish wall paintings, Norwegian tapestries, Finnish drinking vessels and Danish embroidery.

Vasa Museum and Quayside Attractions

As impressive as the Nordiska Museet is, both inside and out, it effectively hides Stockholm's most visited – and most unique attraction. Directly behind the Nordiska you will find the **Vasamuseet** (Vasa Museum; daily June–Aug 8.30am–6pm, Sept–May 10am–5pm, Wed until 8pm; charge; www.vasamuseet.se), the permanent home of the early 17th-century man-of-war *Vasa* warship. Commissioned by King Gustavus II Adolphus on 16 January 1625, it was designed to be the most expensive and richly ornamented naval vessel of its era. However, disaster befell it on its maiden voyage on 10 August 1628 when it capsized and sank in the harbour, soon after being launched. Although its guns were salvaged later that century, the hull lay forgotten until it was discovered in 1956 at a depth of 32m (105ft). The next year salvaging operations were begun, but this very complicated process was not completed until 24 April 1961 when the *Vasa* was sprayed with preservatives and placed in a temporary museum, Wasavarvet, until 1979. In 1963 divers started combing the seabed and, over the five following seasons, rescued numerous artefacts, including hundreds of sculptures. The vessel made its final voyage in 1988 to this creative new museum at Galärvarvet, which was officially opened by King Carl XVI Gustaf on 15 June 1990.

It's best to begin a visit to the *Vasa* by watching the introductory film (shown hourly) or by taking a guided tour (offered several times daily). Afterwards, in this open-plan museum, visitors can inspect, but not board, this amazing vessel from observation platforms on seven levels. Of much interest are the exhibition halls housing ornaments and other

The 17th-century *Vasa* warship

Gröna Lund amusement park

objects from the ship – pottery, coins, pewter tankards, glassware, clay pipes, cannonballs and items of clothing taken from the skeletons of 18 Vasa seamen found on the ship. Among the oddest discoveries were a box containing butter – rancid, of course – and a flask of rum, still drinkable after more than three centuries. Children will especially enjoy 'sailing' the Vasa using computer simulators.

Just behind the museum, moored on the quayside, is the **Museifartygen** (Museum Ships, June–Aug daily noon–5pm; charge) where you can go onboard a steam-powered 1915 icebreaker and a light ship dating from 1903.

The next attraction on the quayside is the compact **Aquaria Vattenmuseum** (Aquaria Water Museum; Falkenbergsgatan 2; mid-June–mid-Aug daily 10am–6pm, rest of the year Tue–Sun 10am–4.30pm; charge; www.aquaria.se), where you will find Nordic and oceanic water environments and a living rainforest. The café has fantastic views over Stockholm.

At Djurgårdsvägen 60 is the **Liljevalchs Konsthall** (Tue–Sun 11am–5pm, Sept–May until 7pm on Tue and Thur; charge; www.liljevalchs.com), which mounts excellent exhibitions of paintings, sculpture and handicrafts.

15 Only a few steps away is **Gröna Lund**, or Tivoli, Stockholm's tasteful amusement park (May–Sept and over Christmas, hours are complicated, so it's best to call ahead; charge; pay for rides separately or buy a discount booklet; tel: 08-587 501 00; www.gronalund.com). In addition to its spectacular setting, rides, roller-coasters, shooting galleries and numerous restaurants, fast-food outlets and bars, it has a first-rate theatre and open-air stage where top Swedish and foreign entertainers perform. While you're still on this side of Djurgårdsvägen, pause to look at the cluster of old houses on some of the narrow streets near the amusement park. This community, known as **Djurgårdsstaden**, was founded more than 200 years ago and grew up around the Djurgårdsvarvet shipyard.

Skansen

Now it's time to cross over Djurgårdsvägen to reach the entrance to **Skansen** (hours vary throughout the year, check website or tel: 08-442 80 00 for details; charge; www.skansen.se), the world's first and most famous open-air museum and a prototype for all the others that followed. Beautifully situated on a 30-hectare (74-acre) hill, it was created by Artur Hazelius in 1891, with the idea of establishing a kind of miniature Sweden, showing how Swedish people, from farmers to aristocrats, lived and worked during different eras.

Some 150 historic buildings from various parts of Sweden constitute an important part of Skansen. They represent a bygone way of life, a culture that started to

Visitors rest in Skansen

Brown bears in Skansen zoo

disappear with the advent of the Industrial Revolution. Gathered here are re-assembled cottages, manor houses, peasant and Lapp huts, and ancient farmsteads, complete with cows, pigs and other farm animals. Country stores and city shops – including a bakery and an old pharmacy – and the 18th-century Seglora Kyrka, popular for weddings, dot the area. Glassblowers, potters, bookbinders and goldsmiths are among the craftsmen plying their trade in the workshops.

It also has a very fine **zoo** featuring northern animals such as reindeer, seals, wolves, deer, bears and the ever-popular *Älg* (elk) in very natural surroundings, as well as fauna from other parts of the world. Look also for a special children's area, Mini-Skansen, with rabbits, kittens, guinea pigs and other small animals, along with botanical gardens, indoor and outdoor restaurants, public dance floors, and an open-air stage that features entertainers of international acclaim. There is also an aquarium and a terrarium with exotic animals, although this admission price is extra.

It is possible that many visitors to Stockholm may not, initially, feel that Skansen is worth a visit; but overlooking this museum would be a major mistake. Skansen is an absolute delight for all ages. There is always something going on and you can easily spend a whole day or more here without any risk of getting bored. The park is also a pleasant spot to visit on summer evenings when there are special programmes, and the view from the hilltop of the lights of Stockholm glittering in all directions off the surrounding waters is spectacular.

Just outside Skansen is the **Biologiska Museet** (Biology Museum; Apr–Sept daily 11am–4pm, Oct–Mar Tue–Fri noon–3pm, Sat–Sun 10am–3pm; charge; www.biologiska museet.com), in an Old Norse-style structure completed in 1893 and built for the Stockholm Exhibition of 1897. It was the first museum in the world to consider exhibiting animals in their natural environs. Its creators were two extremely talented men, the taxidermist Gustaf Kolthoff and the painter Bruno Liljefors.

Here you can admire 300 different species of Nordic animals and birds, including polar bears, Arctic wolves, moun-

Christmas at Skansen

Christmas is a special time at Skansen, where there is a whole month's worth of celebrations and events. The Christmas Market, held on the last weekend of November and the first two weekends of December, has stalls selling all kinds of traditional foods, gourmet items and children's toys and clothes. Besides that, you will find craft demonstrations, live music in some of the old buildings, dancing events and a Christmas workshop where you can make your own Christmas decorations. Of course, the restaurants feature special Christmas menus. Lucia Day is celebrated on 13 December. This festival, known all over Sweden, has Lucia dressed in white and with candles in her hair, arriving in a procession with her attendants. On the last weekend before Christmas there are concerts of Christmas music in the Seglora Church. And the seasonal festivities end when thousands of people arrive at Skansen for celebrations that include evocative music and end with a huge fireworks display.

tain hares and moose, hawk owls, white-tailed eagles and guillemots nesting on cliffs. They are stuffed, of course, but look eerily lifelike in these ingeniously constructed settings. The result is an absorbing museum that is sure to fascinate both children and adults.

Eastern Djurgården

If you don't feel like walking, jump on a number 7 tram or take the 47 bus to **Prins Eugen's Waldemarsudde** (Tue–Sun 11am–5pm, Thur until 8pm; charge; www.waldemarsudde. com). This is the former house and art gallery of Prince Eugen, widely known as Sweden's 'Painter Prince' and one

Prins Eugen's Waldemarsudde

of the most accomplished landscape painters of his generation. When he died in 1947 at the age of 82, he bequeathed his property to the nation. The public can visit the house – where the ground floor offers a fascinating insight into his lifestyle – and the gallery, in a lovely setting of parkland and terraced flower gardens that slope down to a channel of the Baltic Sea. (You can see more of the 'Painter Prince's work at the Gallery of the Prince, used for the city's receptions, in the Stadshuset. Across from windows offering magnificent views of Riddarfjärden, you will find the prince's alfresco painting representing the 'Shores of Stockholm').

Waldemarsudde has an ambitious collection of Swedish paintings, mostly from the late 19th and early 20th centuries. There are also more than 100 works by Prince Eugen. The garden contains a number of first-rate sculptures.

Also on the southern bank of the island is the summer retreat of King Karl XIV Johan. Built in the

See works by Edvard Munch in Thielska Galleriet

1820s, **Rosendals Slott** (Rosendal Palace; June–Aug Tue–Sun guided tours only, on the hour noon–3pm; www.royalcourt.se) was one of Sweden's first prefabricated homes. In 1913 it was opened to the public as a museum devoted to the life and times of the king, and it remains a highly impressive work of historic restoration. The decor is magnificent, with Swedish-made furniture and richly woven textiles in brilliant colours.

Located on the eastern tip of Djurgården, **Thielska Galleriet** (Thiel Gallery; daily noon–4pm; charge; www.thielska-galleriet.se) is a fine collection of turn-of-the-century Scandinavian art in the former home of wealthy banker and visionary collector, Ernest Thiel. The collection includes works by Edvard Munch, Carl Larsson, Anders Zorn and others, many of whom were the banker's friends. The Art Nouveau mansion was designed by architect Ferdinand Boberg, who also designed Prince Eugen's Waldermarsudde and the NK department store. The gallery is one of the few museums open on Monday.

ÖSTERMALM

The attractive and affluent residential area of Östermalm is popular for its many antiques shops and pricey boutiques. One of the most populous districts in Stockholm, it has a distinctly upper-class feel to it, and a bit of window shopping along its broad boulevards is an enjoyable way to pass an hour or two.

Hallwyl Museum and Environs

Just north of the pleasant **Berzeli Park**, dominated by Berns restaurant and bar, is the **Hallwylska Museet** (first-floor state rooms: Tue, Thur–Sun noon–4pm, Wed noon–7pm; charge; guided tours Sat 1.30pm; www.lsh.se). This patrician mansion, completed in 1898, was built for Walter and Wilhelmina von Hallwyl. He came from one of Europe's oldest noble families and she was the daughter of a steel and wood magnate. Wilhelmina was responsible for the amazing collections on display in the 70 perfectly preserved rooms, overflowing with Gobelin tapestries, china figurines, Flemish and Dutch paintings, antique furniture and assorted objets d'art. The mansion was surprisingly modern, with electricity, central heating, hot and cold water, a bath and show-

Inside Hallwylska Museet

er, and even indoor wood-panelled toilets. The Hallwyls donated the house to the state in 1920 and, after Walter's death in 1921, Wilhelmina left complex instructions in her will (including the exact length – to the minute – of tours), as to how the museum was to be run after her death. She died in 1930 and the mansion remains as it was left.

Kungliga Dramatiska Teatern

Further on, at Nybroplan, is the attractive façade of the **Kungliga Dramatiska Teatern** (Royal Dramatic Theatre; www.dramaten.se), where the actors Greta Garbo, Ingrid Bergman and Max von Sydow all began their careers. Before his death in 1953, American playwright Eugene O'Neill bequeathed his last plays to the Dramatic Theatre, and their premieres (including that of *Long Day's Journey into Night*) were staged here.

Just around the corner into Sibyllegatan will take you to the **Musikmuseet** (Tue–Sun noon–5pm; charge; www.musikmuseet.se). This museum is worth visiting just to see the 17th-century Crown Bakery that houses it. First opened in 1901, the museum is a music lover's delight with a unique collection of instruments, a folk music section, workshops and an interactive high-tech sound room.

Just beyond is the **Army Museum** (Tue 11am–8pm, Wed–Sun 11am–5pm, from 10am July–Aug; charge; www.sfhm.se). This museum may not be to everyone's taste. However, it offers a fascinating opportunity to learn about Sweden's complex history in terms of its military and warring past.

Strandvägen

The palatial houses along the fashionable quayside boulevard of Strandvägen (Shore Road) were built in the early 20th century by Stockholm's 10 richest citizens, seven of whom were wholesale merchants. This was a hilly, muddy harbour area until a campaign began in advance of the 1897 Stockholm Exhibition to create a grand avenue unrivalled in Europe. Whether you choose to walk along the central promenade lined with linden trees or beside the quay where the old schooners are anchored, you'll find this is a pleasant stroll.

Museum of National Antiquities

Towards the eastern end of Strandvägen head north up Narvavägen to reach the impressive complex that houses the **Historiska Museet** (Museum of National Antiquities; May–Sept daily 10am–5pm, Oct–Apr Tue–Sun 11am–5pm, Thur until 8pm; charge, guided tours in English at 1pm; www.historiska.se). Ten thousand years of history unfold eloquently in this excellent museum. The 'door of history' at the main entrance, covered with allegorical and historical figures in bronze relief, is the work of the renowned Swedish sculptor, Bror Marklund. The museum has more than 30 rooms, so it's best to pick up a floor plan. The ground-floor exhibits start with artefacts from the earliest inhabitants of Sweden. The Viking Age has yielded a rich collection of gold and silver objects, ornamental art, and weapons and rune stones from the island of Gotland. From a slightly earlier epoch, there is the Treasure of Vendel, a remarkable burial site with the dead in their boats surrounded by everyday objects.

There are magnificent examples of medieval church art on the first floor, including wooden crucifixes modelled on Byzantine art, beautifully painted and sculptured altar pieces, baptismal fonts and gold chalices. One room is devoted entirely to a reconstruction of a typical medieval country church.

The museum's major attraction is the Gold Room, located in a 'rock chamber' some 7m (23ft) below ground level in the museum garden. The circular room displays one of Europe's richest collections of prehistoric jewellery, including gold and silver artefacts dating back as far as AD400.

National Maritime Museum

On the far eastern shore of Östermalm – reached on bus 69, from outside T-centralen subway station in the direction Blockhusudden (alight at Museivägen) – is **Sjöhistoriska Museet** (daily 10am–5pm; charge, free Mon; www.sjohistoriska.se). Located in a fine building designed by Ragnar Östberg, architect of the Stadshuset, this museum traces the history of the Swedish Navy and merchant marines. The centrepiece of the collection is the stern of the schooner *Amphion*, which was instrumental in the

National Maritime Museum

victory of a key battle against the Russian Navy in 1790 under the command of Gustav III.

National Museum of Science and Technology

Near the National Maritime Museum is **Tekniskamuseet** (daily 10am–6pm, Wed until 8pm; charge; www.tekniska museet.se). This museum covers Swedish science and technology through the ages. One of the more fascinating attractions is a reconstructed iron-ore mine in the building's basement. Another is the Royal Model Chamber, displaying the inventions of Christopher Polhem (1661–1751), a genius often described as the 'Father of Swedish Technology'.

SÖDERMALM

⑲ Södermalm is the most youthful and bohemian island in central Stockholm. Once the city's poorest working-class district, it has recently been gentrified and filled with art galleries, boutiques and clubs on top of many places of historic interest. Steep cliffs plunge down into the Baltic and Lake Mälaren, and clusters of rust-red wooden cottages and artists' studios are hidden behind apartment buildings in green areas bordering the sea.

Start at Slussen (the Sluice Gate), a clover-leafed roundabout above the narrow canal connecting the lake with the sea. In the summer months, you'll see many pleasure boats lined up here waiting for the canal lock to be opened. Slussen is home, among other things, to one of the city's most curious sights: **Katarinahissen** (The Katarina Lift; charge). Dating back to 1883, the lift rises in

SoFo

Go to the SoFo area of Södermalm (South of Folkungagatan) for hip independent shops and eateries. Enjoy great food and quirky design at one of the many cafés, or browse the second-hand stores for bargains; www.sofo.se.

Historic homes on Åsögatan in Södermalm

an open shaft to the roof of a tall building, where there is a lovely view of the Old Town from the top.

Fjällgatan, east of the Katarina district, is where most of the city sightseeing buses stop. This little street, perched along the edge of a ridge overlooking the Baltic Sea, provides the visitor with one of the best panoramas of Stockholm. Not far from here there is a charming colony of shuttered, fenced-in cottages grouped on a grassy hill around the Sofia church.

To the west of Slussen there are more picturesque houses at **Mariaberget**. From the heights of Skinnarviksberget, you will experience yet another stunning view of Stockholm, which encompasses sights of Lake Mälaren and Stadshuset.

Hornsgatan, which begins with rows of art galleries in Slussen and ends at the water's edge in Hornstull, is lined with cafés, second-hand boutiques and shops of all descriptions. Check out the vibrant street market in Hornstull during the summer, filled with eclectic stalls and street performances.

OUTLYING ATTRACTIONS

Millesgården

20 One sight not to be missed is **Millesgården** (mid-May–Sept daily 11am–5pm, Oct–mid-May Tue–Sun noon–5pm; charge; www.millesgarden.se), the home, studio and garden of the late Carl Milles (1875–1955), Sweden's famous modern sculptor. Although he lived and worked abroad, mostly in the United States, for long periods, Milles was extremely fond of his place on the island suburb of Lidingö and spent his summers here.

The beautifully terraced sculpture park provides the setting for replicas of Milles' best work. On display are some of his most popular pieces – *Man and Pegasus*, *Europa and the Bull* and the spectacular *Hand of God*. There is also a collection of Greek and Roman sculpture, as well as the work of other sculptors. Millesgården itself is a work of art. Silver birch and pine trees stand guard over statues and fountains, rose beds and urns of flowers, marble columns and flights of limestone steps. Carl Milles died at the age of 80 in 1955, and both he and his artist wife Olga are buried in a small chapel here. Take the underground to Ropsten, then catch a bus

Sculptures in Millesgården

or Lidingö local tram (one stop) to Torsvik.

Haga Park

In the mid 18th century King Gustav III commissioned the architect Frederik Magnus Piper to create a royal park in the popular Haga area of the city. Today **Haga Park** is a national monument and is also home to the **Haga Park Museum** (Tue–Sun 11am–5pm; www.sfv.se) with interesting exhibitions about the park and its buildings.

Haga Park's Sultan Tents

The park is best enjoyed via a stroll down its serpentine paths and – for a real architectural treat – with a visit to the so-called **Sultan's Tents**. Clad in decoratively painted blue and gold copper plate, the Roman-style battle tent exteriors give the desired illusion of a sultan's encampment on the edge of

Ekoparken

Ekoparken is the world's first national city park, a huge set of green lungs which stretch out in a 12km (7-mile) arch from Ulriksdals Slott (Ulriksdal Palace) in the north to the archipelago islands of Fjäderholmarna in the south, encompassing three royal parks, Djurgården, Haga and Ulriksdal. This green land is so large that you need a full day of serious hiking to explore it, by foot during the warmer months or on skis or long-distance skates in winter. A boat trip around the Brunnsviken is an excellent way to tour the Ekopark (winter and summer tours; departs Stallmästaregården hotel and restaurant; www.stromma.se).

a forest. The three tents house the museum, a restaurant and accommodation.

While here, don't miss the opportunity to observe hundreds of exotic birds and butterflies flying freely around the humid greenhouses of the **Fagelhuset** (Bird and Butterfly House).

Museum of Natural History

Green and serene Brunnsviken Bay stretches north into Frescativägen, which is where you'll find the **Naturhistoriska Riksmuseet** (Tue–Fri 10am–6pm, Sat–Sun 11am–6pm; charge; www.nrm.se). Take bus number 40 or 540 to Naturhistoriska Riksmuseet or, if travelling by subway, exit at Universitetet. This huge museum, fronted by a large garden, was established in 1916 and covers various topics of natural history. The museum's biggest attraction is the Cosmonova, the only IMAX theatre in Sweden and one of the most advanced planetariums in the world. Movies in OMNIMAX, the world's largest format, are shown on a huge dome screen above the audience. The films shown are mostly documentaries covering subjects like astronauts in space and unusual aspects of the natural world.

EXCURSIONS

The beauty of its surroundings rivals the beauty of Stockholm itself. To the east are the islands of the archipelago, and to the west is Lake Mälaren, with a collection of castles and towns at the water's edge. There are numerous boat excursions all summer long, on graceful old steamers or fast modern motor launches. Most of those heading for the archipelago will depart from either Strandvägen, across from Dramaten Teater or Strömkajen, near the Grand Hôtel. Stadshusbron, next to City Hall, is the departure point for boats around Lake Mälaren.

Stockholm Archipelago

The Swedes call the Stockholm Archipelago Skärgården, which means 'garden of skerries', and it's a fitting description. Huge and infinitely varied, this hauntingly beautiful archipelago consists of as many as 24,000 rocky islands of all shapes and sizes, extending for some 48km (30 miles) into the brackish waters of the Baltic. There is nothing like it anywhere else in the world *(see also box on page 68)*.

Vaxholm

Vaxholm is an attractive waterfront town in the inner archipelago, reached by way of a charming 50-minute or so cruise aboard one of the boats operated by Waxholmsbolaget (tel: 08-679 58 30; www.waxholmsbolaget.se) or Cinderellabåtarna (tel: 08-120 040 00; www.stromma.se). Waxholm boats set sail from Strömkajen, by the Grand Hôtel and Cinderel-

Taking a boat ride in Vaxholm

la boats leave from Strandvägen. Vaxholm's chief attraction is the 16th-century **Fästnings Museet** (Vaxholm Fortress Museum; June daily noon–4pm, July–Aug daily 11am–5pm, Sept 1st two weekends 11am–5pm; www.vaxholmsfastning.se). On a little island guarding the straits by Vaxholm, this foreboding 16th-century fortress is now the National Museum of Coastal Defence. Vaxholm is a charming place, with waterside paths and plenty of idyllic houses, cafés and restaurants. From the harbour you can watch the motorboats and sailing boats manoeuvring through the narrow channel as they head for more distant points in the Stockholm archipelago.

Sandhamn

Sandhamn is located on a Baltic island at the outer edge of the archipelago. The fastest way there is on a Cinderella Båtarna vessel, which takes 2 hours from Strandvägen (*see page 67*). There is a restaurant/bar on board and you will be able

The Garden of Skerries

In its day the archipelago served as a place of refuge for pirates and smugglers. Later, fishermen lived in unpainted wooden shacks and wealthy noblemen built great estates on many of the islands. The archipelago has now become the favourite playground of Stockholmers that visit their summer holiday houses on weekends or for longer vacations. They sail, fish, swim and sun themselves on the smooth boulders by the water. The archipelago is divided into three distinct sections, each with its own character and special atmosphere. The inner group is made up of larger islands covered with forests and farmland. The middle archipelago consists of a jumble of large and small islands, some with woods and fields of wildflowers, separated by a labyrinth of narrow channels and sounds. The outer archipelago, mostly uninhabited, is a barren seascape of desolate rock islands.

to take in all the diverse and dramatic elements that make up this stunning island world. An important pilot station since the end of the 17th century, Sandhamn is a yachting centre and home of the fashionable Royal Swedish Yacht Club. The tiny, charming village has only about 100 year-round residents, but the figure swells in the summer when tourists and Stockholmers who have summer

Fjäderholmarna, a short boat ride from the city

holiday cottages here invade the island. Sandhamn's summer amenities include several hotels, an old inn, a restaurant with dancing, and good swimming and sailing facilities. In July Sandhamn hosts an international regatta.

Fjäderholmarna

If you prefer not to venture so far into the archipelago, then a trip to the **Fjäderholmarna** (Feather Islands) is for you. Numerous attractions await along with restaurants, bars and even a handicraft village where you can purchase souvenirs. Waxholmsbolaget *(see page 67)* operates frequent sailings from Strömkajen.

Mariehamn

Another fine outing is a cruise to **Mariehamn**, the capital of the Åland islands, comprised of 9,970 sq km (3,850 sq miles) of bays, inlets, islands and skerries located about midway between Sweden and Finland. This autonomous province of Finland has a population of 25,000, most of whom also speak Swedish.

An overnight stop is preferable, though day cruises leave in the morning, stop for a couple of hours in Mariehamn, and are back in Stockholm by late evening. You can also take a 24-hour excursion, sleeping onboard in a comfortable cabin or spending the night in a hotel in Mariehamn. The town has good accommodation facilities and some excellent restaurants.

Travellers on these cruise ships will enjoy a smörgåsbord, and the bars, dance lounges and nightclubs onboard are always lively. Tax-free prices make drinks during the journey less expensive than normal, and since the ships pass through the Stockholm archipelago, you will enjoy a scenic feast as well. For more details, contact the Åland Tourism Board (tel: 358-18 24 000; www.visitaland.com/cruise).

Lake Mälaren

Mälaren is the country's third largest lake, stretching more than 110km (68 miles) west of Stockholm. This area, the Lake Mälaren Valley, has been justly termed the cradle of Swedish civilisation and its most important historic sights are within easy travelling distance from the city via waterways.

Drottningholm Palace

An absolute must, and a most pleasant and rewarding experience, is an excursion to **Drottningholm Palace** (Apr Sat–Sun 11am–3.30pm, daily May–Aug 10am–4.30pm, Sept 11am–3.30pm, Oct Sat–Sun 11am–3.30pm, Nov–Mar Sat–Sun noon–3.30pm; for times of guided tours in English visit the website; charge, gardens free; www.royalcourt.se), situated on a small island in an inlet of Lake Mälaren. A French-style palace built in the late 17th century and described as the Versailles of Sweden, Drottningholm Palace is now the home of the royal family, who live in the south wing (not open to the public). A Strömma Kanalbolaget boat that departs and returns frequently from Stadshusbron (City Hall) will take you through a beautiful stretch of Mälaren and get you there in an hour (tel: 08-12 00 40 00; www.strommakanalbolaget.com).

Drottningholm is a multifaceted attraction. Its extensive gardens, formal in the French style with statuary, fountains and trees, are a delight to walk around. Hidden away to the left of the formal gardens are two very different and very unusual places. The **Kina Slott** (Chinese Pavilion: May–Aug daily 11am–4.30pm, Sept daily noon–3.30pm; guided tours May Sat–Sun noon, 2pm and 4pm, daily June–Aug noon, 2pm and 4pm, Sept daily noon and 2pm; charge), an unusual combination of the rococo and Chinese styles with its two curved wings, is a real anomaly. In fact, when it was designed, no one had any real idea of what a Chinese Pavilion should look like, and as a consequence, this is just a conceptualisation. It was commissioned by King Adolf Fredrik as a surprise gift to his wife, Queen Lovisa Ulrika, on her birthday in 1753. After a complete renovation between 1989 and 1996, it can now be seen in its original state.

The Chinese Pavilion

Very close to it is the even more unusual **Guard's Tent** (May–Aug daily 11am–4.30pm, Sept Tue–Sun noon–3.30pm). Well, it does look just like a tent, but a close-up look tells you some-

Inside Drottningholm Palace

thing different. In fact, it was built in 1781 to serve as quarters for the dragoons of Gustav III, and the intent was to make it look like a 'tent in a Turkish army camp'.

The **Drottningholm Court Theatre** (guided tours on the hour, May–Aug 11am–4.30pm, Sept noon–3pm; charge; www.dtm.se) is adjacent to the palace and is one of the world's most famous theatrical establishments. Not content with this theatre, King Gustav III also constructed a small castle theatre at Gripsholm Slott in the same era. Royal theatres were quite commonplace in Scandinavia, and Copenhagen has its own Court Theatre that dates from 1767. During the summer, this gem of a theatre is the venue for operas by Handel, Gluck, Mozart and others, as well as ballet. The additional touch of musicians dressed up in authentic period costumes and wearing powdered wigs makes you feel as if you're attending a court entertainment some 200 years ago. Before or after the performance, take the opportunity to look at the collections of pictures and costumes tracing the history of stage art, exhibited in the rooms around the auditorium. They include rare Italian and French theatrical designs from the 16th–18th century and original sketches by Gustav III's stage painter. Even if you can't make a performance, then a guided tour is a must.

Birka

A trip to Björkö (Birch Island), one of the lake's 300 islands, should also be considered. This was the site of **Birka**, Sweden's earliest trading centre, where the country's first contacts with Christianity were made in the 9th century. Here St Ansgar built a church and preached to the heathens in the year 830. Obliterated in the 11th century, all that remains of the once-flourishing town of Birka are the faint traces of old fortifications and around 3,000 Viking graves. The island is a pleasant, relaxing place to spend part of a day. Take a guided tour around the **Viking graves** and **excavation sites** or visit the **Birka Museum** (May–Sept; www.raa.se), displaying some of the island's archeological finds. You can reach Björkö in just under 2 hours on a Strömma Kanalbolaget boat that departs and returns from Stadshusbron in the summer.

Birka Museum

Gripsholm Castle

A site that justifies a full day's excursion is Gripsholm Castle, another outstanding attraction at Lake Mälaren. You can be there in an hour and a half by train to Läggesta, followed by a short bus ride. An alternative route by boat, however, is a far more

pleasing proposition. The **SS Mariefred** (tel: 08-669 88 50; www.mariefred.info) is a coal-fired steamer that has been plying the same route since 1903. It makes for a highly memorable trip and you can even enjoy dinner on board. It departs from Stadshusbron, in the summer, at 10am, and returns from Mariefred at 4.30pm, with each trip taking 3½ hours.

At journey's end you'll see the massive, turreted bulk of **23 ▶ Gripsholm Slott** (Gripsholm Castle; mid-May–mid-Sept daily 10am–4pm, mid-Sept–Nov Sat–Sun noon–3pm, rest of year pre-booked groups only; charge; www.royalcourt.se), mirrored like a stage set in the waters of the lake. There was a castle on this site in the 1300s, built by the great Bo Jonsson Grip, but the present structure was built by Gustav Vasa in the 1530s – and subsequently added on to and modified by nearly every succeeding Swedish monarch. The castle served as a state prison at one time, and the deposed King Erik XIV was held captive in its tower. Now a museum, Gripsholm houses one of the largest collections of historical portraits in the world. Don't miss the small **castle theatre** built by Gustav III (who was also responsible for the Drottningholm Theatre), or the two 16th-century bronze cannons in the outer courtyard, seized in wars with the Russians.

Gripsholm Castle

Next door to the castle is **Mariefred**, where the steamer to Gripsholm docks. You may want to pause a while in this attractive little town of yellow and red frame houses, with lovely gardens lined up in tight rows beside narrow streets and a cobblestone square. A white baroque church and an 18th-century town hall are two of the highlights here.

Gripsholm's Russian cannons

Before leaving Mariefred you should take a ride on the **Östra Södermanlands Järnväg** (East Södermanland Railway), a rolling museum of vintage coaches pulled by an old steam engine. This narrow-gauge railway, which dates from 1895, is maintained by local rail buffs. It runs from Mariefred to Läggesta, a distance of 4km (2½ miles). At a top speed of 25km/h (12mph), it's a slow but delightful trip.

Sigtuna

Two other places merit consideration for full day trips. Of these, the closest to Stockholm is **Sigtuna**, situated on a beautiful, slender arm of the lake. Sigtuna, thought to be Sweden's oldest existing town, was founded in 980 by King Erik Segersäll. It served as the religious centre of the country – a role later taken over by Uppsala – and is the site of some of Sweden's oldest churches. It was also Sweden's first capital and a lively trading port until a series of disasters struck. Estonian pirates burned it to the ground; the town gradually recovered, but Gustav Vasa, fired by the ideas of the Reformation, shut down its monasteries and the town fell into obscurity.

The monastery ruins at Sigtuna

Today Sigtuna is a lakeside idyll with the ruins of four churches, built between 1060 and 1130. The 13th-century church of **Mariakyrkan** (St Mary's) remains as testimony to Sigtuna's glorious past. Walk along **Stora Gatan**, said to be the oldest street in Sweden, and have a look at the quaint **Town Hall**, dating from 1744. Other points of interest, aside from the church ruins and scattered rune stones from the Viking era, are the **Sigtuna Museum**, containing local archaeological finds, and the **Lundström House**, a good example of late 19th-century architecture filled with furniture from the same period. The **Sigtuna Foundation**, a Christian retreat and cultural centre, injected new life into the town. It has played host to many prominent authors and scholars who have come here to put the finishing touches to a book or dissertation in the guest rooms that overlook a cloister and rose garden.

Skokloster Castle

25 ▶ Skokloster Slott (May–mid-June Sat–Sun noon–4pm, mid-June–Aug daily 11am–5pm, Sept Sat–Sun noon–4pm, guided tours hourly 12.15–3.15pm; charge; www.lsh.se) is a magnificent baroque palace on the edge of a lovely bay on Lake Mälaren, about 20km (12 miles) northeast of Sigtuna. It was constructed in the latter part of the 17th century by

Carl Gustaf Wrangel, a field marshal under Gustavus Adolphus in the Thirty Years' War. The castle's 100 oversized rooms house a fabulous collection of historical treasures, mostly from the 17th century when Sweden was Europe's preeminent military power. The collection includes silver and glass pieces, tapestries, baroque furniture, over 1,000 paintings and 20,000 rare books and manuscripts, much of it war booty. The arms collection, one of the largest in the world, begins with crossbows and includes such oddities as a set of executioner's swords and a 2.5m (8ft) long rifle that belonged to Queen Kristina. Skokloster's vast estate also has a restaurant, a modern hotel and a **Motor Museum**, with a fine collection of vintage and veteran cars and engines. The prize exhibits are an 1899 Renault, an elegant maroon 1911 Austin and a Spitfire engine from the time of the Battle of Britain.

Uppsala

Uppsala, population 190,000, is 73km (45 miles) north of Stockholm and can be reached in just 40 minutes by train from Centralstationen. This excursion more than justifies an overnight stop.

History jostles you at virtually every corner in Uppsala, an ancient centre of culture, religion and education. It's the seat of the Archbishop of the Swedish Church and home of Uppsala University, one of the world's great institutions of higher learning, which celebrated its 500th anniversary in 1977. It also has a charming atmosphere, with the Fyrisån River meandering its way through the centre of town, a green patina forming on the campus statues, rare and beautiful flowers blooming in the Linnaeus Gardens, and the old wooden buildings ageing gracefully and in sharp contrast to the new glass and steel structures. Most distinctive of all is Uppsala's skyline silhouette; the twin spires of the cathedral and the round towers of the castle are both centuries-old landmarks that dominate the city.

A stop at the Uppsala Tourist Office (Fyristorg 8; tel: 018-727 48 00; www.uppsalatourism.se) will arm you with all the necessary information you will need before you set out to explore the town.

Begin your sightseeing at **Uppsala Domkyrka** (Uppsala Cathedral; May–Sept daily 8am–6pm, Oct–Apr Sun–Fri 8am–6pm, Sat 10am–6pm, with free guided tours on Sun at 12.30pm; www.uppsaladomkyrka.se), right in the middle of the university grounds. This massive 13th-century cathedral with its lofty 122-m (400-ft) spires was completed over a span of 150 years. Many famous Swedes are buried here: King Gustav Vasa (and his three wives); St Erik – Sweden's patron saint and king who died a martyr in Uppsala in 1160; Emanuel Swedenborg, mystic, scientist and philosopher; and Carl Linnaeus, the botanist who, like Swedenborg, worked at Uppsala University. The **Treasury Tower Museum** (May–Sept daily 10am–5pm, from 12.30pm Sun, Oct–Apr daily 10am–4pm from 12.30pm Sun; charge) contains religious tapestries, articles of silver and gold and other objects of great historical and aesthetic interest.

Uppsala Cathedral

Pause to look at the medieval wall paintings in the **Trinity Church** (Helga Trefaldighetskyrkan), which celebrated 700 years of existence in 2002, before you

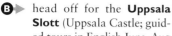

B head off for the **Uppsala Slott** (Uppsala Castle; guided tours in English June–Aug daily 1pm and 3pm; charge; www.uppsalaslott.com). Construction of this looming red structure, on a hill overlooking the town, began in the 1540s under Gustav Vasa. The castle has been the setting of lavish coronation

Castle cannons

The cannons at Uppsala Slott are aimed directly at the cathedral. This is because when Gustav Vasa severed ties with the Pope he intended the castle to be the symbol of royal power and he wanted to intimidate the archbishop and clergy.

feasts and many dramatic historic events. It was here, for instance, that Gustavus Adolphus held the talks that led Sweden into the Thirty Years' War, and that Queen Kristina gave up her crown in 1654 before setting off for Rome. Today Uppsala Castle is home to the **Uppsala Konstmuseum** (Uppsala Museum of Art; Tue–Fri noon–4pm, Sat–Sun noon–4.30pm; charge), which exhibits contemporary art.

Of the university buildings, the most notable is **Carolina Rediviva** (Mon–Fri 8.30am–9pm, Sat 9am–6pm; www.ub.uu.se), which houses the biggest and oldest library in Sweden, founded by Gustavus Adolphus in the 17th century. The collection contains 5 million books and half a million manuscripts and documents, many from medieval times. Among them are extremely rare items, including the Codex Argenteus (Gothic Silver Bible), written in the 6th century in silver letters and gold capitals on purple parchment.

Drop into the **Gustavianum** (Tue–Sun 10am–4pm; charge; www.gustavianum.uu.se), a university building topped by a most curious room; an octagonal anatomical theatre under a striking dome. It was built in the 1620s by Olof Rudbeck, one of many brilliant scientists who have taught and conducted research here. Now home to the University Museum, it contains an exhibit on early anatomical and medical studies, Nordic and

Linnéträdgården

Egyptian antiquities and – a real gem – the thermometer of Anders Celsius.

Many people travel to Uppsala simply to visit places connected with Carl Linnaeus, famous as the 'Father of Modern Botany'. Linnaeus came to Uppsala in 1728 as a medical student, was appointed lecturer in botany after only two years at the university, and became a professor of medicine in 1741. Linnaeus named and described some 10,000 different species of plant. Some of these species can be seen in the university's **Linnéträdgården** (May–mid-Sept daily 11am–8pm; museum: 11am–5pm; charge; www.linnaeus.uu.se), which houses 1,300 plants arranged according to species, exactly as in Linnaeus's era. His home in the gardens is now a museum and is open to the public.

During the summer, botanists lead groups of visitors on marked trail walks following the footsteps of Linnaeus in the forests around Uppsala. You can also visit **Hammarby**, Linnaeus's summer home 15km (9 miles) from Uppsala, where he received hundreds of students from all over the world. The garden here is said to contain a number of specimens planted by Linnaeus himself (park: May–Sept daily 11am–8pm; museum: May and Sept Fri–Sun, June–Aug Tue–Sun 11am–5pm; charge).

Continuing with this theme, the **Botaniska Trädgården** (Botanical Garden; daily May–Sept 7am–9pm, Oct–Apr 7am–7pm, gardens free; Orangery: Tue–Fri 9am–3pm, free; Tropical Greenhouse: May–Sept Tue–Fri 9am–3pm, Sat–Sun noon–3pm, charge; www.botan.uu.se) is a must-see for those with such interests. Over 13,000 different species and sub-species from around the world are found here, including tropical plants, and Mediterranean trees and shrubs in the Tropical Greenhouse and Orangery.

Be sure to make the excursion to **Gamla Uppsala** (Old Uppsala), about 3km (2 miles) out of town and reached by bus from the city centre. This is the site of the ruins of a pagan temple and three huge burial mounds said to contain the remains of kings mentioned in the epic *Beowulf*. The graves, dating from the 6th century, are called Kungshögar-na (Kings' Hills). A 12th-century parish church stands on the remnants of the heathen temple where human and animal sacrifices were offered up to the gods. (Museum: Apr and Oct Mon, Wed, Sat–Sun noon–3pm, May–Aug daily 11am–4pm; charge; www.raa.se/olduppsala). Close by is Odinsborg restaurant and café, where you can drink mead *(mjöd)* from old Viking ox-horns.

Walpurgis Night

Uppsala is a picture of tranquility for 364 days of the year, but there is one day when all of the suppressed emotions explode into a burst of colour and noise. This happens on the last day of April every year, with the traditional half-pagan and half-Christian celebration called *Valborgs-mässoafton* (Walpurgis Night). The celebrations begin in the afternoon when undergraduates and their friends gather in front of the Carolina Rediviva and await a signal from the rector of the university before donning their white student caps and letting out a huge cheer. Later in the evening the whole university – students, professors and alumni – march with flaming torches and the flags of the 'nations' (nations, in this context, are the students' clubs that represent the different Swedish provinces) up to Castle Hill where they burst into songs hailing the country and the arrival of spring.

WHAT TO DO

SHOPPING

Shopping in Stockholm is a delightful entry into the world of design. Top products include glassware, ceramics, stainless-steel cutlery, silver, furniture and textiles. Sweden's fine reputation in these fields rests on old traditions of skilled craftsmanship passed down through generations. Contemporary Swedish design has its roots in the peasant art of the past.

Stockholm offers a broad range of shops and department stores. Most shops open from 10am until at least 6pm on weekdays, but close early on Saturday, normally at 4pm. Many shops, all department stores and most shopping malls are also open on Sundays. The two city-centre malls, Sturegallerian and Gallerian, open from 11am–5pm.

Where to Shop

There are three large **department stores** in the centre. Prestigious Nordiska Kompagniet (NK) at Hamngatan 18–20 is Stockholm's classic department store and a city landmark. PUB is located on the corner of Drottninggatan and Kungsgatan, at Hötorget, and stocks less expensive

Clothes shopping in Filipa K's vintage shop

Tax tip

'Moms' is Sweden's equivalent of VAT, a 25 percent tax on most products and services. Visitors from outside the EU can reclaim this on leaving Sweden. When buying in shops displaying the blue-and-yellow 'Tax-Free Shopping' sticker, present your passport and you will be given a form which can be redeemed at the tax-free service counter in ports, airports and on ships. Note that refunds apply for a limited period after purchase.

fashions and quality homewares. Åhléns City at Klarabergs-gatan 50, is Sweden's largest department store, also known for its inexpensive, quality homewares and food department.

For fun shopping in a medieval milieu, try exploring **Gamla Stan**. Västerlånggatan, the pedestrian street bisect-ing the island, and the lanes surrounding it are lined with shops, boutiques and restaurants.

Stockholm's **main markets** are the colourful Östermalm-storg, an indoor market noted for its cheese and fish spe-cialities, and Hötorget, a lively outdoor market where the locals buy their food from Monday to Saturday and shop for books, crafts and bric-a-brac on Sunday.

Södermalm has trendy design shops as well as antiques and second-hand shops, particularly around Götgatan, Hornsgatan and Folkungagatan streets. In summer, Horn-stull's Street market offers an eclectic mix of stalls, cafés and street performance.

Best Buys

Ceramics. Rörstrand and Gustavsberg are the predomi-nant names in this field, but there are many smaller com-panies. The wide choice ranges from fanciful items that easily fit in your suitcase to one-of-a-kind sculptures with a price tag to match their considerable size. If you are vis-iting a ceramic factory, you may find something suitable below shop prices.

Christmas decorations. For Swedes, Christmas is a time of strong tradition, and Yuletide ornaments are frequently very attractive. Larger department stores, having realised the dec-orations' potential as souvenirs, are today offering tourists a small selection of these splendid items all year round.

Clogs. These traditional wooden Swedish shoes, called *träskor*, have become popular in many parts of the world. They are available in Stockholm's shops in a wide range of designs.

Designer clothes. If you're looking for up-market shops, you should head for Grev Turegatan, Biblioteksgatan, Birger Jarlsgatan and Norrmalmstorg in Östermalm. Here are exclusive international labels, including Gucci and Prada, alongside local talented designers such as Filippa K and Johan Lindeberg.

Designer jewellery. L'etui, Birger Jarsgatan 7, tel: 08-611 05 77, www.letui.se, is a small shop where you will find a fascinating array of jewellery designed by Per Eric Berggren, hand crafted at his workshop just outside town.

Food. Just before you leave Stockholm, don't forget to buy a selection of Swedish cheese, herring, caviar, smoked salmon, crispbread and a bottle of aquavit, the popular throat-burning national drink.

Glassware. This is one of Sweden's most famous design products. Names such as Orrefors and Kosta Boda are recognised worldwide, and talented artists and artisans working

Brandstaton vintage store in bohemian Södermalm

Swedish glassware

for these and other companies consistently produce inventive designs. Nordiska Kristal is the best for glassware and has shops in Gamla Stan at Österlånggatan 1, tel: 08-10 77 18, and a main shop and art gallery downtown at Kungsgatan 9, tel: 08-10 43 72, www.nordiskakristall.com.

Home furnishings. Like the other Scandinavian countries, Sweden is famous for its emphasis on design – especially on furniture and products for the home, ranging from affordable high street shops like Hemtex, Lagerhaus and Duka, to more exclusive stores like the Design Torget (www.designtorget.se) and Svenskt Tenn (www.svenskttenn.se).

Knitwear. Kilgren, Våsterlånggatan 45, Gamla Stan, tel: 08-20 94 24, www.kilgren.se, is an long-established shop selling a wide range of Nordic sweaters, Scottish kilts and cashmeres and hand-made traditional knives. Oleana, Järntorget 83; tel: 08-10 26 22; www.oleana.no, is a Norwegian company that produces beautifully designed women's sweaters and cardigans.

Lapp handicrafts. Although Stockholm is a long way from Lappland, many shops sell a range of knife handles, pouches and other goods handcrafted out of reindeer antlers and skins.

Silver. Silversmiths fashion innovative necklaces, bracelets and rings, as well as stunning silver bowls, cigarette cases, etc.

Souvenirs. Brightly painted, red, hand-carved Dala horses, named after the province of Dalarna, are probably the most typical and popular of Swedish souvenirs. Other typical souvenirs are painted linen tapestries, knitwear and handmade dolls. Svensk Hemslöjd (The Swedish Handicraft Society), Norrlandsgatan 20, tel: 08-23 21 15, www.svenskhemslojd. com, has genuine handicrafts from across Sweden.

Sporting goods, hunting and outdoor wear. The Swedes are renowned for their excellent camping equipment, as well as the fishing rods and reels made by ABU, a Swedish company that has become one of the world's biggest exporters of high-quality fishing gear. Widforss, Fredsgatan 5, tel: 08-466 05 10, www.widforss.se, is an institution in Stockholm, where you'll find guns, fishing equipment, boots, Barbour waterproofs and Victorinox knives.

Stainless tableware. Swedish cutlery, or flatware, is not only beautiful, but makes a fine gift that is easy to carry home.

Suede. Coats, jackets and even skirts made out of suede are excellent buys in Stockholm. Suede, in fact, is a Swedish invention, and also is the French word for Sweden.

Colourful Swedish souvenirs

What's on?

An indispensable guide to what's happening in the city, *What's On?*, is published each month by the Stockholm Visitors Board, and is available free at hotels and many other places. You can also visit www.visitstockholm.com for events listings.

ENTERTAINMENT

The entertainment possibilities in Stockholm may not be equal to those of, say, New York or London, but enough goes on in this town to satisfy the desires of any visitor. Moreover, the long, light Stockholm summer nights are made-to-order for relaxing outdoor activities.

Music and Theatre

The massive auditorium of the Stockholm Konserthuset (www.konserthuset.se) is the principal venue for music performances during the winter months, the season stretching from September to May or June. In summer you can enjoy concerts in a variety of splendid settings scattered throughout the Stockholm area – the Royal Palace, the courtyard of the Hallwylska Museet, Prince Eugen's Waldemarsudde, St Jacob's Church and the German Church in the Old Town. There are also open-air concerts in many of the city parks, including Kungsträdgården in the heart of town.

First-rate opera and ballet are offered at Operan (Royal Opera; www.operan.se) from early autumn to late spring. In summer the Drottningholm Court Theatre *(see page 72)* stages 17th- and 18th-century drama.

Modern and classical plays are staged at Kungliga Dramatiska Teatern (Royal Dramatic Theatre; www.dramaten.se) and Stadsteater (Stockholm Municipal Theatre; www.stadsteatern.stockholm.se), although in Swedish only. The Marionette Theatre (tel: 08-506 201 01) mounts puppet and marionette productions suitable for children and adults.

Top venues for jazz are the Stampen, a pub in the Old Town, Fasching on Kungsgatan, and the Lydmar Hotel. The Stockholm Jazz Festival is held in July on Skeppsholmen. From Abba to the Hives, Sweden continues to produce successful pop and rock acts. An increasing number of venues host live events: check the local press for details of upcoming shows.

Cinema

There are many cinemas in the city centre, and most foreign films are shown in their original language with Swedish subtitles. Check the free newspapers available in the *tunnelbana* (subway) or one of the other local newspapers.

Nightlife

Most nightclubs, including a few at hotels, now open until 3am, and in some cases until 5am. Many have live dance music; some also offer cabaret and variety shows. If you sit at a table you are expected to eat; at the bar ordering food is unnecessary. In addition to nightclubs, there are also dance restaurants in town that close earlier, at around 1am. Note that though the cost of drinking has fallen a little in recent years, a night on the town can still be expensive.

For the most happening clubs and bars visit www.stockholmtown.com.

Live rock music is popular

Skansen Park

Parks

The famous open-air museum of Skansen *(see page 53)* has a full and varied summer season of outdoor entertainment. This may include anything from a performance by an orchestra to a foreign dance troupe.

Another focal point of summer entertainment is Skansen's close neighbour, Tivoli Gröna Lund *(see page 52)*, on the shore of Djurgården. Crowds flock to the amusement park's open-air stage to be entertained by international performers.

SPORTS

The Swedes are a very sports-minded people, so it's not surprising that the Stockholm region boasts excellent sporting facilities. Top spectator sports are soccer (in the summer) and ice hockey (in the winter). Prestigious sporting events, such as the ice hockey championships, are held in the Globe Arena, whose gigantic white dome you may have noticed on the city's south horizon. Reputed to be the largest spherical building anywhere in the world, the Arena can be transformed rapidly from a sports stadium into a theatre or a concert hall. For the brave, it also features the SkyView, with glass pods that carry passengers up the exterior of the building.

Water sports such as sailing, swimming, water skiing, windsurfing, canoeing and fishing are very popular, as you would expect in a city that virtually floats on water. Swedes are also fond of jogging, hiking and cross-country skiing and there are many trails for these activities in nearby wooded areas.

A number of recreational facilities are located in Djurgården, where you can rent a bike, go horse riding and enjoy promenading. Get in touch with the Stockholm Visitors Board, www.visitstockholm.com, for up-to-date information on sports around the city. The following is a round-up (in alphabetical order) of the sports facilities on offer in and around Stockholm.

Canoeing. Sweden is well-equipped for canoeists. Visit www.kanot.com for detailed information on locations and canoe hire facilities. The sheltered waters of the Stockholm archipelago are also good for sea kayaking. (for more information see www.visit-stockholm.com).

Fishing. Pollution has been eliminated from Stockholm's waters over the past few

The Globe Arena sports venue

Sailing through Stockholm

years, and it's now possible to fish for salmon in Strömmen, the stream that flows past the Royal Palace. There is good fishing in Lake Mälaren, in the smaller lakes in the city environs and around the 24,000 islands of the archipelago in the Baltic Sea. A fishing permit is not required in the city, but is elsewhere (Fiskeriverket, Fisheries Department; tel: 031-743 03 00; www. fiskeriverket.se).

Golf. Golf is a popular summertime activity. In the Stockholm area the following golf courses stand out: Djursholms Golfklubb, tel: 08-544 964 50, www.dgk.nu; and Saltsjöbadens Golfklubb, tel: 08-717 01 25, www.saltsjobadengk.se.

Hiking. There are plenty of easy, marked walking trails, which start just outside Stockholm. The summer trails are indicated by raised or painted stones and all-season trails by crosses. Ambitious hikers can follow a trail called 'Upplandsleden' from Järfälla to Uppsala and from Bålsta to Enköping. To the east of Stockholm, the trail called 'Roslagsleden' extends 56km (35 miles) between Danderyd and Domarudden.

Sailing. During the summer there are numerous boats on Lake Mälaren, in the archipelago and skimming through the city's waterways. There are at least ten places in the Stockholm area where boats can be rented (again, check with the tourist office) and special harbours for visitors with their own boats. However, sailing through the labyrinth of islands that make up the Stockholm archipelago is not to be attempted by amateurs.

Skating. The most popular and conspicuous outdoor rink is in Kungsträdgården in the centre of town. However, many Swedes prefer long-distance skating along the frozen waterways of Lake Mälaren and the Baltic Sea in winter, when the ice is thick enough. Skates can be hired from most popular locations.

Swimming. In the Stockholm region there are 200km (125 miles) of beaches – both sea and lake bathing – including several at Riddarfjärden, near the city centre. One of the most pleasant pools is Vanadisbadet, near Sveavägen, which has been converted into a water park. For a truly relaxing bathing experience, complete with sauna or a massage and beauty treatment, try one of the elegant indoor establishments. Sturebadet, in the Sturegallerian (tel: 08-545 01500; www.sturebadet.se) or Centralbadet, Drottninggatan 88 (tel: 08-545 213 13; www.centralbadet.se).

Tennis. Two of the best venues, with indoor and outdoor courts, are Tennisstadion, tel: 08-545 252 54, www.tennisstadion.se; and Kungliga Tennishallen, tel: 08-459 15 00 www.kltk.se. For those who enjoy watching the game, the Stockholm Open is held in October.

Sightseeing by canoe

STOCKHOLM FOR CHILDREN

Stockholm is a city with a large number of family activities appealing to all ages. One major children's attraction is the archipelago's countless islets, for boating, swimming and fishing. However, there are many other highlights to occupy children.

With a Stockholm Card, three children under seven may be included for free when accompanied by an adult *(see page 131)*.

Aquaria: At this water museum in Djurgården, children can follow the course of a rainforest river from the mountains to the open sea, among other attractions *(see page 52)*.

Junibacken: Home to Astrid Lindgren's Pippi Longstocking and other storybook characters. Worth the steep entrance fee. (Galärparken, Djurgården; Tue–Sun 10am–5pm; tel: 08-587 230 00; www.junibacken.se.)

Gröna Lund: This amusement park, only open during the summer, has many rides and other activities *(see page 52)*.

Skansen: This open-air museum is perfect for families, with a mix of animals (including petting zoo, aquarium and crocodile pond), historical buildings and cafés *(see page 53)*.

Tekniskamuseet (Technical Museum): Older children will be fascinated *(see page 62)*.

Ride at Gröna Lund

Leksaksmuseet (Toy Museum): Displays interesting toys. (Tegelviksgatan 22; Mon–Fri 10am–5pm, Sat–Sun 11am–4pm; tel: 08-641 61 00; www.leksaksmuseet.se.)

Kulturhuset Kid's room: On the fourth floor of the Kulturhuset *(see page 38)* are three children's 'book' rooms, with hammocks and hideaways. Best of all, it's free.

Calendar of Events

The Swedes may be modern in their social and sexual attitudes, but they are very traditional when it comes to celebrations. Throughout the year, festivals brighten up the calendar. (For a comprehensive list of public holidays in Sweden; *see page* 128)

30 April: Valborg or Walpurgis Night has its roots in Viking times. Huge bonfires blaze across the landscape, saluting the arrival of spring. The university towns are especially exuberant; students hold torchlight parades and toast spring in verse, speeches, and songs *(see page* 81*)*.

1 May: May Day, a statutory holiday. Political marches usually held. June: On Archipelago Boat Day (1st Wed in June) numerous steamboats make their way over to Vaxholm Island.

6 June: The Swedish National Day is celebrated with flags and parades. There is a ceremony when the king and Royal Family (Queen Silvia in Swedish national costume) present flags to honour organisations and individuals.

Friday between 20 June and 26 June: On the longest day of the year (Midsummer Eve), colourful maypoles decorated with garlands of birch boughs and wildflowers are raised in village and town squares all over Sweden. Dancing, along with a fair amount of drinking and merrymaking, continues far into the night, which in midsummer is as bright as day. In Stockholm, anyone can join the Midsummer Eve festivities at Skansen.

September: Lidingöloppet, the world's largest cross-country race, is held at Lidingö.

10 December: A week of cultural and scientific events culminates in Nobel Prize Day when the prestigious prizes are given at a ceremony in the Stockholm Concert Hall.

13 December: One of the winter highlights is St Lucia Day. Young girls dressed in long white gowns are crowned with wreaths of lighted candles that symbolise light breaking through the winter darkness. They sing a special Lucia song and serve saffron buns, *glögg* (mulled wine) and coffee.

EATING OUT

The best way to describe the Swedish approach to food is 'natural'. A Swede can become quite lyrical at the thought of *färskpotatis*, a dish of new potatoes boiled with dill (a commonly used herb in Sweden) and served with a pat of butter. Wild berries and mushrooms are highly prized, especially since food prices are high. Swedish law gives everyone the right, known as *allemansrätten*, to wander through fields and forests to pick these gifts of nature. Even city dwellers, never too far away from the great outdoors, take the opportunity to gather *smultron* (wild strawberries), *blåbär* (blueberries), *hjortron* (Arctic cloudberries), *svamp* (mushrooms) and *lingon* (wild cranberries).

In Sweden each season has traditional specialities, and any discussion of eating habits must take these into account. Some regional dishes, such as blood soup and fermented herring, may sound less than appetising, but those visitors with adventurous palates will want to try at least a few of those foods that time-honoured custom prescribe.

Blueberry picking

Where to Eat

Stockholm offers a great variety of dining establishments. Recent years have brought pizzerias, burger chains, international restaurants and the obligatory Hard Rock Café (Sveavägen 75; www.hardrock.se). The real problem nowadays is finding genuine, old-fashioned Swedish food.

Look for restaurants serving *husmanskost* – traditional Swedish dishes, such as *Janssons frestelse* (Jansson's Temptation), a delicious casserole of potatoes, anchovies, onion and cream; *Kåldolmar*, stuffed cabbage rolls; *pytt i panna*, diced meat, onions and potatoes; *kalops*, beef stew; *dillkött*, lamb or veal in dill sauce; *köttbullar*, the famous Swedish meatballs; *sill*, herring pickled in salt or various sauces; *strömming*, fried, boned herring from the Baltic sea; and on Thursdays, join almost all locals in eating *ärter med fläsk*, yellow pea soup with pork, followed by *pannkakor med sylt*, pancakes with jam.

Swedish meatballs

The *smörgåsbord* can be hard to find sometimes, except on Sunday afternoons and during the Christmas season. Strömma Kanalbolaget's brunch boat tour serves a tasty smörgåsbord (tel: 08-12 00 40 00). Otherwise, ask your hotel receptionist for advice.

Eating out in Stockholm is not cheap, but prices at the top-flight restaurants are in line with comparable establishments in other European cities. There are many inexpensive self-service cafeterias throughout the city, and most restaurants have small portions for kids at reduced prices. Look for the *Dagens rätt* (dish of the day), usually excellent value at lunch time. Remember that some restaurants may be closed during July.

Lunch is served around noon, and dinner from 6pm. A service charge is normally included in the restaurant bill, though the waiter or waitress may also hope for a small extra tip – maybe 10 percent if you are satisfied with the service.

Breakfast and Bread

A Swedish breakfast *(frukost)* usually consists of a cup of coffee or tea with slices of bread, butter and and marmalade, and cheese. Other toppings might include slices of ham or salmon, with maybe some lettuce and tomato. A much more substantial breakfast with eggs, bacon, or ham will certainly be available at your hotel where a breakfast buffet is almost always included in the price.

Swedish breakfast

Coffee – which is excellent in Sweden – is consumed in great quantities at all times of the day and night, and forms a recognised part of Swedish social life. The Swedes also drink a lot of milk with their meals. In addition, yogurt and other kinds of fermented milk are popular.

Be sure to try *knäckebröd* (crisp rye bread), which comes in a wide selection and is something worth taking back home, along with some cheese: there are more than 200 different cheeses to choose from. Look for *vasterbottenost*, *herrgårdsost* and *sveciaost* – these are typical hard, well-aged cheeses.

Spring and Summer Fare

As the name implies, *fettis-dagsbullar* or *semlor* (Shrove Tuesday buns) are associated with Lent, but they are now so popular that they appear on the market right after Christmas. The baked buns are split, filled with an almond paste and whipped cream, and are sometimes served in a deep dish with hot milk, sugar and cinnamon. The arrival of spring is traditionally celebrated with an-

Färskrökt lax with potatoes and dill

other calorie-packed treat, *våfflor* (crisp waffles served with jam and whipped cream), as well as three salmon delicacies – *gravad lax* (pickled salmon in dill served with mustard sauce), *färskrökt lax* (smoked salmon) and *kokt lax* (boiled salmon),

Summertime means almost 24-hour daylight in Sweden. It's a season when people can luxuriate in fruit and vegetables that have been grown locally under the midnight sun, instead of the expensive imported produce available during much of the year. Look for *västkustsallad*, a delicious seafood salad that also contains tomatoes and mushrooms.

A delightful custom not to be missed by anyone visiting Sweden in August is the *kräftor* (crayfish) party. This is when Swedes abandon all rules of table etiquette as they attack mounds of small lobster-like creatures gleaming bright red in the light from gay paper lanterns strung above the tables. *Kryddost* (spiced cheese), buttered toast and fresh berries complete the traditional menu. The mood can become quite festive as liberal amounts of snaps *(aquavit)*

Visit Östermalmhallen to sample Swedish delicacies

are usually downed on this occasion. This highly potent drink accompanies another seasonal speciality, *sur-strömming* (fermented Baltic herring). Indeed, many people can't get this fish past their nose without the aid of a dram or two of aquavit. The smell, to put it mildly, is staggering. Even so, some Swedes, particularly those that come from the northern part of the country, consider the dish a great delicacy.

Autumn and Winter Fare

Although southern Sweden is the best place to celebrate St Martin's Day, you can usually find restaurants that observe the tradition in Stockholm as well. The star of this November event is *stekt gås* (roast goose), but the first course and dessert probably deserve the most attention. You begin the meal with a highly spiced *svartsoppa* (blood soup) and finish with *spettekaka*, a lace-like pyramid cake baked on a spit: it melts in your mouth.

The Christmas season gets off to an early, charming start in Sweden on 13 December – one of the darkest and shortest days of the year – when Lucia makes her early-morning appearance in many homes and even in public places. Dressed in a long white robe, with a crown of lighted candles on her head, the Queen of Light awakens the sleeping house by singing the special Lucia song and serving saffron buns, ginger snaps and coffee.

Christmas is preceded by weeks of preparation in the kitchen. Though no longer the feast it once was, the Yuletide smörgåsbord *(julbord)* still retains its essential ingredients. Restaurants also often make a special feature of the smörgåsbord around the holidays.

However, the smörgåsbord is only part of the Swedish holiday menu. Other dishes are *lutfisk* (cod that has been dried and cured in lye), *risgrynsgröt* (rice porridge that contains one almond destined to be found by the person to be wed in the coming year) and some *skinka* (ham). This time of year also brings forth all kinds of delicious breads and pastries.

The Smörgåsbord

Bounded by the sea and with some 96,000 lakes dotting its countryside, Sweden has an abundant supply of fish, which naturally plays an important role in the country's diet. In the old days fish was often dried, smoked, cured or fermented to preserve it for the winter. Even today, in the age of the deep freeze, these methods are still among some of the favourite ways of preparing herring and other treasures from the sea. The herring buffet, or sillbord, the predecessor of the smörgåsbord, is still the basis of Sweden's most famous culinary attraction.

The smörgåsbord table (or groaning board, if you will) can consist of as many as 100 different dishes. It should not be tackled haphazardly. The first thing to remember is not to overload your plate – you can go back for more as many times as you wish.

Even more important is the order in which you eat. Start by sampling the innumerable herring dishes, taken with boiled potatoes and bread and butter. Then move on to other seafood, like smoked or boiled salmon, smoked eel, Swedish caviar and shrimp. Next come the delightful egg dishes, cold meats (try the smoked reindeer) and salads. The small warm dishes are next – meatballs, fried sausages and omelettes – and finally, finish with sweets, cheese and fruit.

Alcoholic Beverages

Teetotaller organisations are a powerful factor in Swedish politics and this has led to very high taxes on alcoholic beverages, especially hard liquor, in order to discourage drinking. Also, with the exception of a very weak beer that can be bought in grocery stores or supermarkets, alcohol is sold only by Systembolaget, the state-owned liquor monopoly.

Systembolaget stores, recognisable by a green-and-yellow rectangular sign, do stock a vast range of recognised brands of whisky, vodka, gin, and so forth, but wine is by far the best value for your money. The stores usually open Mon–Fri 10am–6pm and Sat until 2pm, and you have to be 20 years of age to purchase alcohol.

Sweden's national drink, aquavit (or snaps), is distilled from potatoes or grain and flavoured with herbs and spices, coming in many varieties. Aquavit should always be consumed with food, especially herring; it should be served ice-cold in small glasses, swallowed in a gulp or two and washed down with a beer or mineral water. When you see a bottle with the word LINE on it, you'll know it's special stuff. In the old days, barrels of aquavit went with the

Skål! A glass of aquavit

sailors and they swore that it tasted better after having returned from a voyage that had crossed the equator. These days the custom is continued. Barrels are specially sent to cross the line, and when they return the liquor is bottled and the details of the voyage are detailed on the back of the label, and can be read through the bottle.

Other specialities include *glögg*, a hot, spiced wine at Christmas, and *punsch* (punch), which is usually served after dinner, well-chilled, with coffee.

TO HELP YOU ORDER ...

beer	**öl**	menu	**matsedeln/**
bread	**bröd**		**meny**
butter	**smör**	milk	**mjölk**
cheese	**ost**	mineral	
coffee	**kaffe**	water	**mineralvatten**
cream	**grädde**	potatoes	**potatis**
dessert	**efterrätt**	sandwich	**smörgås**
fish	**fisk**	soup	**soppa**
fruit	**frukt**	sugar	**socker**
ice cream	**glass**	tea	**te**
meat	**kött**	wine	**vin**

MENU READER

ägg	egg	**lök**	onion
biff	beef steak	**matjessill**	pickled herring
böckling	smoked herring	**morot**	carrot
fläskkotlett	pork chop	**musslor**	mussels, clams
gädda	pike	**nyponsoppa**	rosehip soup
jordgubbar	strawberries	**oxstek**	roast beef
kalv	veal	**paj**	pie
kassler	smoked pork	**räkor**	shrimps
korv	sausage	**renstek**	roast reindeer
köttbullar	meatballs	**rödspätta**	plaice
krabba	crab	**rotmos**	mashed turnips
krusbär	gooseberries	**skaldjur**	shellfish
kyckling	chicken	**skinka**	ham
lammstek	roast lamb	**sparris**	asparagus
lax	salmon	**spenat**	spinach
lever	liver	**vitkål**	white cabbage

PLACES TO EAT

We have used the following symbols to give an idea of the price for an evening meal for two without wine:

€€€€ over 1,000kr   €€ 300–500kr
€€€ 500–1,000kr   € below 300kr

MODERN STOCKHOLM

Berns Asian €€€ *Berzeli Park, tel: 08-566 322 22, www.berns. se.* Daily, breakfast, lunch and dinner. Opened in 1863 – with an opulent 19th-century interior open-air veranda, this was a renowned restaurant and cabaret spot for over 100 years. Redesigned by Terence Conran, it is now a delightful restaurant and bar complex. The restaurant offers the best of modern Asian cuisine.

The Bull and Bear Inn €€–€€€ *Birger Jarlsgatan 16, tel: 08-611 10 00. www.bullandbear.se.* Monday to Friday dinner, Saturday and Sunday lunch and dinner. Authentic English pub, with typical pub food combined with a huge selection of draught and bottled beers and over 200 types of malt whisky.

Café Opera €€€ *Operahuset, tel: 08-676 58 07.* Monday–Saturday lunch and dinner. Meeting place for Stockholm's artistic elite ever since it opened in 1905. Art Deco interior with comfortable leather armchairs and marble-topped tables. Home-cooked Swedish dishes and, in 2011, it revived the tradition of the weekend smörgåsbord from May to August.

GQ Restaurang €€€€ *Kommendörsgatan 23, tel: 08-545 67 430, www.gqrestaurang.se.* Tuesday to Saturday dinner only. Opened in August 2005, the owner/chef, Jürgen Grossman, has experience in several top-class restaurants. Lovely low-key dining areas where you can choose from the Menu GQ, a Swedish menu or an asparagus menu and fantastic cheeses from Philippe Olivier in France.

Grill €€€–€€€€ *Drottninggatan 89, tel: 08-31 45 30, www.grill.se.* Monday to Friday lunch and dinner, Saturday and Sunday dinner only. The colourful décor here in the large dining area is so varied that it resembles a furniture showroom, and that is exactly what it is – as everything is for sale. You can choose from five types of grill – *forno al legno* (brick oven), barbecue, charcoal, rotisserie and *ishiyaki* – with some dishes cooked at your table. The restaurant bar attracts the trendy young.

Halv Grek Plus Turk € *Jungfrugatan 33, tel: 08-665 94 22, www.halvgrekplusturk.se.* Monday to Friday lunch and dinner, Saturday and Sunday dinner only. Situated on a quiet corner in Östermalm, open daily and offering excellent value dishes from the eastern Mediterranean region. The generous meze dishes are recommended.

Hermans € *Fjällgatan 23B, tel: 08-643 94 80.* Daily lunch and dinner. Vegetarian home cooking in a cosy atmosphere, with imaginative, organic, all-you-can-eat buffets at lunchtime and in the evening, plus a vegetarian barbecue when weather permits. Large outdoor patio with terrific views of Gamla Stan and the harbour. Live bands play soul, jazz and bossa nova throughout the summer.

Kungshallen € *Kungsgatan 44, tel: 0708-655 620, www.kungshallen.nu.* Monday to Friday breakfast, lunch and dinner, Saturday and Sunday lunch and dinner. Near Hötorget, this is reputed to be Scandinavia's largest food hall. With 14 restaurants catering to very different tastes, there's bound to be something here to suit everyone. Take-aways also available.

Lux €€€€ *Primusgatan 116, tel: 08-619 01 90, www.luxstockholm.com.* Tuesday to Friday lunch and dinner, Saturday dinner only. With one of the newest Michelin stars in Stockholm, this restaurant is found on one of the smaller islands a short taxi ride from the city centre. Located in the old Electrolux factory building that has been transformed into a beautiful example of Scandinavian design. The specialities are modern, innovative dishes based on homegrown traditions.

Mathias Dahlgren €€€€ *Södra Blasieholmshamnen 6, tel: 08-679 35 84, www.mathiasdahlgren.com.* Renowned masterchef Mathias Dahlgren uses the best Swedish ingredients to create elegant, unusual, melt-in-the-mouth dishes in his two restaurants at the Grand Hotel. Matbaren has one Michelin star; Matsalen has two. The food is complemented by exceptional wines, most of which are served by the glass. Superb.

Operakällaren €€€€ *Operahuset, tel: 08-676 58 00, www.operakallaren.se.* Daily, dinner only, closed July. A venerable institution, dating back some 200 years, with a dining room considered the most beautiful in Sweden. The restaurant is a member of the prestigious Les Grandes Tables du monde. It has a magnificent wine cellar considered the best-stocked in the country, while pike, char and langoustine are highlights of the menu.

PA & CO €€–€€€ *Riddargatan 8, tel: 08-611 08 45, www.paco.se.* Daily, dinner only. This restaurant has earned a reputation for innovation that attracts many regulars and guests of local importance to savour its delicacies. No reservations taken, so be sure to get there early.

Restaurang 1900 €€€ *Regeringsgatan 66, tel: 08-20 60 10, www.r1900.se.* Monday to Friday, lunch and dinner, Saturday, dinner only. On the corner with Brunnsgatan, this achingly trendy restaurant and cocktail bar is the baby of well-known Swedish TV chef. He honours his native cuisine with dishes such as halibut and scallops, all elegantly prepared.

Stadshuskällaren €€€–€€€€ *Stadshuset, tel: 08-506 322 00, www.profilrestauranger.se.* Found in the basement of City Hall, come here to savour a Nobel Banquet under beautiful arched ceilings. In fact, your dinner will consist of the menu and wines served to the Nobel Prize winners the previous 10 December. Excellent personal service.

T/bar €€€ *Strandvägen 7C, tel: 08-459 68 02, www.diplomathotel.com.* Daily, lunch and dinner. A modern, stylish restaurant located on the ground floor of the Hotel Diplomat with views over the water. Interesting mixed menu ranging from club sandwiches to poached smögen cod with scampi.

The Veranda €€€ *S. Blaiseholmshamnen 8, tel: 08-679 35 86, www.grandhotel.se*. Daily, breakfast, lunch and dinner. No one should leave Stockholm without trying a smörgåsbord at this delightful restaurant in the Grand Hôtel, which looks out over the Royal Palace across the water. A little brochure provides helpful explanations on smörgåsbord etiquette and brännvin (also known as akvavit). A small bottle of the house special, 1874 Grand Aquavit, particularly smooth for this fiery drink, comes with the meal.

Victoria €€ *Kungsträdgården, tel: 08-21 86 00, www.vickan.nu*. Daily, lunch and dinner. Situated on the lively Kungsträdgården this is a good value option for its location. Try classic Swedish meatballs or the delicious fish and seafood casserole. On balmy summer nights there are plenty of outside tables from which to soak up the lively atmosphere.

Wedholms Fisk €€€–€€€€ *Nybrokajen 17, tel: 08-611 78 74, www.wedholmsfisk.se*. Monday to Friday lunch and dinner, Saturday dinner only. Considered by many to be Stockholm's premier seafood restaurant, and holder of a Michelin star. A plain but distinguished dining room. No ingredients or presentation can compete with the fish – the freshest and most varied selection in town. Bar has an extensive wine cellar.

GAMLA STAN (OLD TOWN)

Bistro Ruby €€€ *Österlånggatan 14, tel: 08-20 57 76, www.grillruby.com*. Daily, dinner only. Saturday brunch from 1pm–5pm. A lovely, intimate old-style Swedish dining room that has a romantic atmosphere. It serves Swedish dishes with a French flavour.

Den Gyldene Freden €€€–€€€€ *Österlånggatan 51, tel: 08-24 97 60, www.gyldenefreden.se*. Monday to Saturday, lunch and dinner. Stockholm's most prestigious restaurant, it opened in

1772 and was named the 'Golden Peace' after the peace treaty with Russia in 1721. The Swedish cuisine, superb service, and original atmosphere are not to be missed.

Djuret €€€ *Lilla Nygata 5, tel: 08-506 400 84 www.djuret.se.* Monday to Saturday, dinner only. The restaurant's name means 'animal' and is an apt choice because the concept here is to only serve one animal at a time, in its various cuts, then change the menu to accommodate another meat. It's a novel idea, devised to encourage sustainability, but it's also quite fascinating to see quite how much variety can be gained from one beast.

Fem Små Hus €€€ *Nygränd 10, tel: 08-10 87 75, www.fem smahus.se.* Classic Stockholm restaurant famed for both its cooking and atmosphere, situated close to the Royal Palace in the cellar vaults of a hotel of the same name. Beautifully prepared dishes include platters of assorted herring, filets of reindeer with cranberries and port wine sauce, oven-baked salmon with white wine sauce and delicious berry desserts.

Frantzén/Lindeberg €€€€ *Lilla Nygatan 21, tel: 08-20 85 80, www.frantzen-lindeberg.com.* Tuesday to Saturday, dinner only, closed July. Only the freshest of ingredients are used here, at one of Stockholm's newest 'foodie' venues, which means that the menu changes almost daily. But with that, each day is a surprise – snails with caviar, chocolate with sea salt – taste sensations abound.

Järnet Matsal & Bar €€–€€€ *Österlånggatan 34-36, tel: 08-10 71 37, www.jarnet.nu.* Monday to Saturday, lunch and dinner. Select from a small but varied menu in this unpretentious, charming restaurant. Enjoy the aroma of prawns being flambéed by your table.

Kryp In €€–€€€ *Prästgatan 17, tel: 08-20 88 41, www. restaurangkrypin.nu.* Monday to Friday dinner only, Saturday and Sunday lunch and dinner. Tucked away on a quiet side street, this is a small, but charming restaurant with a great atmosphere where you will find a good selection of attractive and tasty traditional Nordic cuisine.

1132

Tid: 13:36:07
Kassa: 21

0018   CINDOR LITET   25,00 kr
                    5 å 5,00 kr
1009000   FRIMÄRKE, inom Sverige   60,00 kr
                    10 å 6,00 kr

            Moms 25%   17,00 kr

TOTAL   85,00 kr

Mottaget Kontant   100,00 kr
Åter Kontant   15,00 kr

Tack för att du besökte
Vasamuseet
Välkommen åter!

VASA
MUSEET

Vasamuseet
Butiken
Galärvarvsvägen 14
115 21 Stockholm
08-51954800
Org nr.: 202100

Nr: 63105
Datum: 2013-10-1
Kassör: 21

103

Mårten Trotzig €€€–€€€€ *Västerlånggatan 79, tel: 08-442 25 30, www.martentrotzig.se.* Monday to Friday dinner only, Saturday and Sunday lunch and dinner. Trendy, elegant restaurant named after a 16th-century German businessman and set around the courtyard of an ancient building. Small menu of first-rate fish and meat dishes. For a less expensive meal, try the bar menu.

Pontus by the Sea €€€ *Tullhus 2, Skeppsbron, tel: 08-20 20 95, www.pontusfrithiof.com.* Monday to Friday lunch and dinner, Saturday and Sunday dinner only. Found in the old Gamla Stan Bryggeri, and on the quayside of Skeppsbron, this has a more lighthearted Mediterranean flavour and ambiance than its more established sister restaurant, Pontus!, at Brunnsgatan 1. The quality of the food remains excellent.

Reisen Bar & Matsal €€–€€€ *Skeppsbron 12, tel: 08-22 32 60, www.firsthotels.com.* Monday to Friday, lunch and dinner, Saturday to Sunday dinner only. Found within the First Hotel Reisen, and with delightful views over the water, this has an interesting traditional menu – and the advantage of being open on Sunday evening too. Also has an attractive bar.

Siam € *Stora Nygatan 25, tel: 08-20 02 33, www.siam restaurant.se.* Monday to Saturday, lunch and dinner, Sunday dinner only. The only Thai restaurant in Gamla Stan and located, incongruously, in 17th-century cellars.

Stortorgskällaren €€€ *Stortorget 7, tel: 08-10 55 33, www. stortorget.org.* Daily, lunch and dinner. Choose from either brick-lined cellars or a large covered terrace overlooking the ancient square, you can taste traditional Swedish cuisine that changes seasonally.

Trattoria Romana €€€ *Mälartorget 15, tel: 08-796 90 09.* Daily, lunch and dinner. A long-time favourite amongst politicians. Beautifully decorated with Italian artwork lining the walls and serving excellent, authentic Italian food (a shipment of fresh goods is imported from Italy to the kitchen every week).

RIDDARHOLMEN

Mälardrottningen €€–€€€ *Riddarholmen, tel: 08-545 18 780, www.restaurangmalardrottningen.se.* Tuesday to Friday, dinner only. International and Swedish cuisine is served on the Mälardrottningen, once the American socialite Barbara Hutton's luxury yacht, which is now permanently docked on the Riddarholmen quayside. Excellent, varied dishes. On a clear evening, dining on the open deck offers one of the best views of Stockholm.

SÖDERMALM

Bauer €€ *Götgatan 15, tel: 08-640 08 20.* Monday to Saturday, lunch and dinner. The gimmick here is a Swedish play on tapas and meze – small dishes, ideal for those who want a quick bite while taking in the local shops, or the chance to order a variety for different tastes and flavours.

Gondolen €€€ *Stadsgården 6, tel: 08-641 70 90, www.eriks.se.* Monday–Saturday, lunch and dinner. Located in Slussen at the top of the Katarina Lift, this fine restaurant is a tourist attraction in its own right. The cuisine and views equal each other with their excellence.

La Cucaracha €€ *Bondegatan 2, tel: 08-644 39 44, www.la cucaracha.se.* Daily, dinner only. Tucked away in the interesting section of Stockholm, this is a typical, and fine, Spanish restaurant with an enticing selection of tapas, single or combination plates, desserts and wines and beers.

UPPSALA

Domtrappkällaren €€–€€€ *Sankt Eriksgränd 15, tel: 018-13 09 55, www.domtrappkallaren.se.* Monday to Saturday, lunch and dinner. French, Italian and Swedish cuisines served in a cellar dating from the 14th century. Located near the cathedral. Specialities include delicious salmon and reindeer, as well as other fresh game dishes. Good-value lunch available. Reservations necessary.

A–Z TRAVEL TIPS

A Summary of Practical Information

A

ACCOMMODATION *(hotell; logi;* see also CAMPING, YOUTH HOSTELS and the list of RECOMMENDED HOTELS on page 136)

Hotels in Stockholm have a reputation for cleanliness, facilities, good service, but rather small rooms, regardless of their price category. In reality, however, the majority of hotels are what would be considered, if there were a standardised rating system, three- or four-star class, and thus not inexpensive. It is always advisable to book accommodation in advance, and not just in high season as Stockholm is a year-round conference destination. You can ask for the hotels in Sweden brochure at the Swedish tourist office in your country or check out www.hotelsinsweden.net. The website, www.visitstockholm.com, operated by the Swedish Visitors Board (SVB), has a free online hotel booking service along with detailed information on hostels and campsites. **Hotellcentralen**, also operated by the SVB, is located at Centralstationen (Central Station), tel: 08-508 285 08, and offers free advance booking of hotels, hostels and special city and weekend packages (Mon–Fri 9am–6pm, Sat 9am–4pm, Sun 10am–4pm). Bookings can also be made at the **Stockholm Tourist Centre** on Hamngatan; however, they are subject to a reservation fee. There is an unmanned automatic hotel reservation system at Arlanda airport.

The **Stockholm à la carte** hotel package is worth consideration; www.destination-stockholm.com. From 540kr per person you can choose from 54 hotels in a range of prices and the package includes accommodation, breakfast and the Stockholm à la carte card – which provides free entry to various attractions and free public transport. The package can be booked all days of the week from mid-June to mid-August and on weekends and holidays the rest of the year.

Some hotel chains operate plans of their own, or in conjunction with other groups, enabling you to get certain discounts.

Arrange bed and breakfast accommodation in Stockholm by contacting: **Bed & Breakfast Agency**, tel: 08-643 80 28, www.bba.nu;

Bed and Breakfast Center, tel: 08-730 00 03, www.stockholm-bed-and-breakfast.se; or **Bed and Breakfast Service**, tel: 08-660 55 65, www.bedbreakfast.se.

I'd like a...	Jag skulle vilja ha ett...
single room	**enkelrum**
double room	**dubbelrum**
I have a reservation.	**Jag har beställt rum.**

AIRPORTS *(flygplats)*

Arlanda (ARN) is Stockholm's main airport (tel: 08-797 60 00; www.arlanda.se), located 41km (26 miles) from the city. The airport has four terminals: numbers 5 and 2 are for international flights, and numbers 3 and 4 for domestic flights. Inter-terminal buses and walkways transfer passengers between the terminals.

Ryanair flies into both **Skavsta** (NYO) (tel: 0155-28 04 00; www.skavsta.se) and **Vasterås** (VST; tel: 021-805 600; www. stockholmvasteras.se) airports, both about an hour and 20 minutes by bus from the centre of town

Bromma (BMA), Stockholm's City Airport (tel: 08-797 68 00; www.brommaairport.se) is closer to town and handles more than 1 million people every year to and from other parts of Scandinavia.

The fastest way between Stockholm's Centralstationen (Central Station) and Arlanda airport, just 20 minutes' distance, is on the **Arlanda Express train**, tel: 08-588 890 00, www.arlandaexpress. com. These run every 15 minutes between 5am and midnight and the fare is 460kr return. Beware, though, there is a 50kr surcharge if you wait to purchase the ticket on the train. **Airport buses** *(Flygbussarna*; tel: 08-588 228 28; www.flygbussarna.se) shuttle between the City terminal and all airports, and are the cheapest option. **Taxis** are very expensive, but insist on the fixed rate that varies between 350–425kr.

B

BICYCLE HIRE (cykel)

Between April and October **Stockholm City Bikes** (tel: 077-444 24 24; www.citybikes.se) is a scheme that allows you to pick up and drop off bikes at stands throughout the city. Bike cards, from the tourist office and other outlets, cover three days (165kr) or the whole season (300kr) but the maximum loan per session is three hours between 6am and 10pm. You can also rent a bicycle at **Cykel & Mopeduthyrning**, Strandvägen, Kajplats 24, tel: 08-660 79 59.

BUDGETING FOR YOUR TRIP

The following are some approximate prices in Swedish kronor (kr) to help you plan your travelling budget.

Flights. Low-cost airlines can cost as low as 400kr return from the UK to Stockholm; scheduled flights are more likely to be in the region of 3,500kr return. The earlier the booking the lower the price is likely to be.

Hotels. In general prices for hostel accommodation start at around 350kr. Mid-range hotel rooms can be found for around 800–1,000kr but it's not unusual for prices to be as high as 2,000kr and above for more high-end hotels (see also pages 112 and 136).

Meals. Continental breakfast in a restaurant/café costs around 70kr; lunch 100–150kr; dinner at a medium-priced restaurant (not including drinks) 300kr per head. Look for the sign Dagens rätt (dish of the day): salad, a main course and coffee, which is usually good value. Dagens rätt is served weekdays, generally between 11am–2pm.

Drinks. Coffee or soft drinks cost upwards of 30kr. Alcohol is expensive: a bottle of wine will cost at least 150kr; spirits (4cl) 75kr, except aquavit which is 50kr. Any alcohol over 3.5 percent has to be bought at Systembolaget, a state-run chain of stores (see page 102).

Museums. Entry to many city museums is free. Those that do charge cost 50–100kr. Most are free or offer reduced rates to under-18s.

C

CAMPING

The closest camping grounds to Stockholm are **Bredäng Camping**, Stora Sällskapets Väg 51, 12731 Skärhomen, tel: 08-97 70 71; www.bredangcamping.se, which is 10km (6 miles) southwest of the city centre and also has cabins and dorm-style accommodation, and **Ängby Campsite**, Blackebergsvägen 25, 16852 Bromma, tel: 08-37 04 20, with 200 pitches for caravans or tents.

Cabins. These can be hired throughout the archipelago. For information contact **Hotellcentralen** (see page 112).

CAR HIRE (biluthyrning; see also BUDGETING FOR YOUR TRIP)

In reality, visitors to Stockholm and the numerous attractions in its immediate vicinity, will find that having a car is more of a hindrance than an assistance. The public transport system is superb and the numerous boats that ply the waters of the archipelago and Lake Mälaren are an attraction in their own right. Besides that, car hire, like petrol, is not inexpensive, with an average minimum overnight rate of 1,000kr, and the penalties for speeding and other restrictions are severe.

However, notwithstanding that, if you are planning to tour around the country, or just feel you want a car, then hiring a car before you go can avoid any uncertainties. There are **Avis**, **Rent a Car**, **Europcar**, **Budget** and **Hertz** car hire offices at Arlanda Airport.

If you decide to hire once you are in Stockholm, then you can contact **Avis**, tel: 010-49 48 050; **Europcar**, tel: 0771-387 67 227; **Budget**, tel: 08-503 833 333; or **Hertz**, tel: 08-797 99 00. These are toll free numbers and can only be dialled within Sweden.

The legal minimum driving age in Sweden is 18, but to hire a car you need to have held a licence for three years so, in practice, the minimum age is 21. Drivers under 25 usually have to pay a premium. You'll need your driving licence and passport. Most companies require a deposit, but this is waived if you present an accepted credit card.

CLIMATE AND CLOTHING

Climate. Most of Sweden has a continental climate, with a medium to large temperature difference between summer and winter. In summer temperatures rise above 20°C (70°F). Summer is, of course, the prime season to visit Stockholm. In midsummer, daylight lasts up to 19 hours, with lots of sunshine – and lots of other visitors. In spring, which is particularly lovely in the lake district and outlying regions, and autumn, with bright colours and clear nights, you'll have Sweden to yourself. Winter is tempting for sports enthusiasts and Christmas in Sweden can be an unforgettable experience.

The following chart will give you an idea of the average daily temperatures and average number of rainy days each month in Stockholm.

	J	F	M	A	M	J	J	A	S	O	N	D
Max °F	31	31	37	45	57	65	70	66	58	48	38	33
Min °F	23	22	26	32	41	49	55	53	46	39	31	26
Max °C	-1	-1	3	7	14	18	21	19	14	9	3	1
Min °C	-5	-6	-3	0	5	9	13	12	8	4	-1	-3
Days of rainfall	10	7	6	7	7	8	9	10	9	9	10	11

Clothing. Although the weather is usually very pleasant during the day in the short summer months, it cools enough at night to make a sweater or light jacket necessary. The weather can be unpredictable, so pack a light waterproof coat. In the spring and autumn thicker clothing will be required, while in winter warm boots, coat, hat, gloves and scarf are necessary. Appropriate shoes are also needed as visiting the Old Town and other parts of Stockholm require much walking, often on cobbled streets.

Stockholmers no longer dress up as they used to, and even at the theatre or opera, smart casual clothes are the norm. There are a few late-opening restaurants that expect guests to wear a jacket and tie.

CRIME AND SAFETY (See also EMERGENCIES AND POLICE)

Sweden is one of the safest countries in the world. Nevertheless, like other cities, Stockholm has kept up with the times, which means that crime has increased. And although you are not likely to get mugged, there are warnings in hotels advising visitors not to leave bags unattended in the breakfast rooms and restaurants. This, obviously, is good policy anywhere and it is also good policy to check your valuables – including passport and airline tickets – into the hotel safe. Another sensible precaution is to take photocopies of passports and airline tickets and keep them separate from the originals. In instances where the originals are stolen, lost or damaged this will save an enormous amount of time and hassle. When the pubs close on Saturday night, it tends to be rowdy and can be unpleasant.

Any loss or theft should be reported at once to the nearest police station, if only for insurance purposes; your insurance company will need to see a copy of the police report.

Call the police.	**Ring polisen**
My ... has been stolen.	**... har stulits**
passport	**mitt pass**
handbag	**min handväska/**
wallet	**min plånbok**
Help!	**Hjälp!**

D

DRIVING (See also CAR HIRE)

Drive on the right, pass on the left. Traffic on main roads (and very often main streets in town) has the right-of-way. Speed limits are always indicated by signs, but as general guidance the limits are 50km/h (30mph) in urban areas, 70km/h (43mph) outside towns and cities and 110km/h (70mph) on motorways. Traffic on roundabouts usually has priority, but in other situations traffic from the right has right-of-way. Give way to pedestrians at official pedestrian crossings and any cyclist crossing a cycle track. Drink driving is a serious offence and police are free to stop motorists and breathalise at will. You can be fined or even sent to jail if your alcohol level exceeds (20mg per 100ml of blood).

International pictographs are widely used, although you may see some signs in Swedish. Note that a Swedish mile is equal to 10km.

Breakdown assistance can be obtained by calling **Assistancekåren**, tel: 020-912 912, or **Falck**, tel: 08-731 69 03, provided you have pre-arranged the service with your own recovery organisation such as the AA or the RAC prior to your holiday.

Parking in the city centre can be difficult and expensive but there are a number of municipal car parks and metered parking. Better

car registration papers	**besiktningsinstrument**
Where's the nearest filling station?	**Var ligger närmaste bensinstation?**
Please check the oil/tyres/battery.	**Kan ni kontrollera oljan/däcken/batteriet, tack.**
I've broken down.	**Bilen har gått sönder.**
There's been an accident.	**Det har hänt en olycka.**
How do I get to ...?	**Hur kommer jag till ...?**

biljettautomat	ticket machine
bussfil	bus lane
busshållplats	bus stop
ej genomfart	no through traffic
privat parkering	private parking
enskild väg	private road
körkort	driving licence
motorväg	motorway (expressway)

yet are the park and ride schemes that allow parking an transport hubs and journeys into the centre by public transport.

E

ELECTRICITY

The supply for electric appliances in Sweden is 220 volt, 50 Hz AC, and requires standard two-pin, round continental plugs. Visitors should bring their own adapters.

EMBASSIES

Embassies, with consulate sections, are generally open Monday to Friday 8.30am–4.30pm, but there is usually a 24-hour telephone service in operation. New Zealand does not have an embassy in Sweden.

Australia: Klarabergsviadukten 63, 8th Floor, SE-101 36, Stockholm, tel: 08-613 2900, fax: 08-613 29 82, www.sweden.embassy.gov.au

Canada: Klarabergsgatan 23, 6th Floor, 103 23 Stockholm, tel: 08-453 3000, fax: 08-453 3016, www.canadainternational.gc.ca

Republic of Ireland: Hovslagargatan 5, 111 48 Stockholm, tel: 08-5450 4040, fax: 08-660 13 53, www.embassyofireland.se

South Africa: Fleminggatan 20, 4th Floor, 112 26 Stockholm, tel: 08-24 39 50, fax: 08-660 71 36, www.southafrica.se

UK: Skarpögatan 6-8, Box 27819, SE-115 93 Stockholm, tel: 08-671 30 00, fax: 08-662 9989, www.britishembassy.se.

US: Dag Hammarskjölds väg 31, SE-115 89, Stockholm, tel: 08-783 53 00, fax: 08-661 19 64, www.usemb.se.

EMERGENCIES (See also POLICE AND HEALTH AND MEDICAL CARE)

The general emergency telephone number in Sweden is **112**. This covers the ambulance *(ambulans)*, rescue service, fire department *(brandkår)*, police *(polis)*, as well as air/sea and mountain rescue services, the poison hot line and on-call doctors. It can be dialled free of charge (no coins needed) from any telephone. English is usually understood.

G

GAY AND LESBIAN TRAVELLERS

Sweden is one of the world's most progressive countries when it comes to gay rights. Since 1988 government legislation has granted gay relationships the same status as heterosexual marriages and the state has given financial support to gay organisations. Information and advice can be obtained from the **Swedish Federation for Lesbian and Gay Rights:** RFSL (Riksförbundet för Sexuellt Likaberätti-gade), Stockholms Gay Centre, Sveavägen 59 (postal address: Förbundskansli, Box 350, 10126 Stockholm), tel: 08-501 62 900, www.rfsl.se. **QX** (www.qx.se) is a gay/lesbian magazine that offers information about clubs, restaurants, bars and shops mainly in Stockholm, Gothenburg, Malmö and Copenhagen.

GETTING THERE

By Air

From the UK: There are direct flights from the UK to Stockholm from London Heathrow and London City with **British Airways**, tel: 0844 493 0787, www.british-airways.com; from London Heathrow with **SAS (Scandinavian Airlines System)**, tel: 0871 226 7760, www.sas.se; and from London Gatwick with **Norwegian Airlines**, tel: 721 49 00 15, www.norwegian.se. SAS and Norwegian also fly direct from Edinburgh.

From the US: SAS operates daily flights to Stockholm from New York Newark and Chicago. Continental Airlines, tel: 800-231 0856, www.continental.com also flies to Stockholm from Newark and Delta Airlines, tel: 1-800 221 1212, www.delta.com, from New York John F Kennedy (JFK).

Although several other airlines fly directly to Stockholm, an interesting option is to fly **Icelandair**, tel: 800 223 5500, www.iceland air.com, who have services from New York, Baltimore/Washington, Boston, Orlando, Minneapolis St Paul and San Francisco to Reykjavik, Iceland, with connections on to Stockholm which allow a stop-over in Iceland, too.

From Europe: There are direct flights to Stockholm from many destinations including France, Germany, Greece, Portugal and Spain.

From Australia and New Zealand: There are no direct flights from these countries. Depending upon the city of destination, Qantas operates flights to Stockholm in conjunction with other airlines that necessitate one or two, sometimes three, changes, usually in the Far East and then Europe. Air New Zealand operates flights from Auckland to London and then from London on another airline to Stockholm.

From South Africa: South African Airlines does not operate flights to Stockholm, but there are a number of daily flights between London and Stockholm.

By Rail

Stockholm, on the eastern coast of Sweden, is easily accessible by rail from Copenhagen, Denmark and Oslo, Norway, but connections to Helsinki, Finland, are best made by way of a direct ferry, or a ferry to Turku, Finland, and then by train.

Rail Passes. Rail Europe, tel: 08448-484 064, www.raileurope. co.uk, offers the InterRail One Country Pass offers train travel within Sweden on three, four, six or eight days within a one month period. Eurail, www.eurail.com, offers a similar pass for non-European citizens, with discounts for travellers under the age of 26. as well as a Scandinavia Pass, which covers Sweden, Denmark, Norway and Finland and is valid for two months.

By Sea

There are no longer direct ferries from the UK to Sweden, but DFDS Seaways, tel: 0871 522 9955, www.dfdsseaways.co.uk, operates a route from Harwich to Esbjerg in Denmark. From here it's a drive of some 900km (560 miles), or there is a train from Esbjerg to Copenhagen and another on to Stockholm.

GUIDES AND TOURS *(guide)*

The **Stockholm Tourist Service** operates a private guide and group booking service (tel: 08-1200 49 79; www.stotourist.se), and books transport and authorised guides for individuals and groups. Approximately 30 languages are catered for, and the minimum fee is 2,320kr for up to 3 hours. You can also book specially trained taxi drivers who serve as guides. The taxi guides are available in approximately 10 languages.

Stockholm Sightseeing (tel: 08-1200 40 00, www.stromma.se) offers several boat tours of the city, including the two-hour 'Under the Bridges of Stockholm' tour, which takes in both the Baltic Sea and Lake Mälaren sides of Stockholm and offers multilingual commentary. Tours depart on the hour from Strömkajen, just in front of the Grand Hôtel. They also offer a variety of bus tours, including Stockholm Panorama, which lasts 1½ hours, has multilingual commentary and departs from Gustav II Adolfs Torg, in front of the Royal Opera House, almost every hour in summer. Two hop-on-hop-off bus tours cover the southern side and northern side of the city respectively.

H

HEALTH AND MEDICAL CARE *(See also* EMERGENCIES*)*

Medical Care. No vaccinations are needed for entry to Sweden. EU residents should obtain the European Health Insurance Card, available from post offices or online at www.ehic.org.uk, which entitles them to emergency medical and hospital treatment and has replaced the E111 form for UK travellers. Citizens of non-EU countries should ensure they have adequate travel/health insurance before leaving home.

If you fall ill, have an accident or are in need of a doctor, call or go to **CityAkuten**, Apelbergsgatan 48, ('T' Hötorget) tel: 020-150 150, between 8am and 6pm Monday to Friday, or ask someone such as your hotel receptionist to call a doctor for you. Make sure the doctor is affiliated with *Försäkringskassan* (Swedish National Health Service).

If you are able, go to a hospital's emergency and casualty reception *(akutmottagning)*; take your passport with you for identification. Any prescriptions need to be taken to a chemist *(apoteket)*. A 24-hour health care information service can be reached at tel: 08-32 01 00.

Chemists/pharmacies *(apoteket)* stock over-the-counter products like cough medicine and aspirin and also supply prescriptions. A 24-hour pharmacy service is offered by **C.W. Scheele** at Klarabergsgatan 64 near the Centralstationen (Central Station), tel: 0771-450 450 (this is also the number for general pharmacy information throughout Sweden). Nevertheless, it is a good idea to bring along an adequate supply of any prescribed medication from home.

Precautions. Tap water and ice are perfectly safe to drink throughout Sweden. In summer midges can be a problem so insect repellent is advised.

Where can I find a doctor who speaks English?	**Var kan jag få tag på en läkare som talar engelska?**
I am ill.	**Jag är sjuk.**

L

LANGUAGE

English is widely spoken and understood all over Sweden, and for the most part, no English-speaking person visiting the country will have any trouble at all communicating in English. Children study English at school from the age of nine.

Although Swedish is a pleasant language to hear, you are unlikely to find it easy to pronounce. Remember there are three extra letters in the Swedish alphabet, å, ä and ö, which appear after the usual 26 letters (something to bear in mind when looking up a name in the telephone book).

Sunday	söndag	Thursday	torsdag
Monday	måndag	Friday	fredag
Tuesday	tisdag	Saturday	lördag
Wednesday	onsdag		

0	noll	16	sexton
1	ett	17	sjutton
2	två	18	arton
3	tre	19	nitton
4	fyra	20	tjugo
5	fem	21	tjugoett
6	sex	30	trettio
7	sju	40	fyrtio
8	åtta	50	femtio
9	nio	60	sextio
10	tio	70	sjuttio
11	elva	80	åttio
12	tolv	90	nittio
13	tretton	100	(ett) hundra
14	fjorton	1,000	(ett) tusen
15	femton		

yes/no	ja/nej	here/there	här/där
hello/		old/new	gammal/ny
goodbye	hej/hejdå	good/bad	bra/dålig
please/thanks	tack	early/late	tidig/sen
big/small	stor/liten	cheap/expensive	billig/dyr
quick/slow	snabb/långsam	right/wrong	rätt/fel
entrance/exit	ingång/utgång	near/far	nära/långt
open/shut	öpen/stängd	hot/cold	varm/kall

January	**januari**	July	**juli**
February	**februari**	August	**augusti**
March	**mars**	September	**september**
April	**april**	October	**oktober**
May	**maj**	November	**november**
June	**juni**	December	**december**

M

MAPS

Free maps of Stockholm are available from any of the city's tourist offices.

MEDIA

Radio and television. Sveriges Radio (Radio Sweden) and Sveriges Television (Swedish Broadcasting Corporation) used to have a monopoly on all radio and television programmes transmitted in Sweden. Now, however, there are also privately owned radio stations and television channels. Sveriges Radio broadcasts regular 30-minute programmes of news and information in English, which can be heard over most of Sweden on medium wave 1179KHz (254m), and also in the Stockholm area on FM 89,6MHz. Further details are available from Radio Sweden International, SE-105 10 Stockholm, tel: 08-784 50 00, or from many hotels. Two of the country's five TV channels, SVT1 and SVT2, are financed through licence fees, while the others accept advertisements. In addition to Swedish channels, most hotels now carry English-language satellite channels – from the US and UK, as well as other international stations.

Newspapers and magazines *(tidning; tidskrift)*. Sweden's main daily newspapers are *Svenska Dagbladet*, *Dagens Nyheter* and *Göteborgs Posten* (the latter two are broadsheets) and *Expressen* and *Aftonbladet* (these are tabloids), all in Swedish. *The Interna-*

tional Herald Tribune and British papers, as well as a wide variety of magazines, are sold at the Central Railway Station, airport shops, hotels, tobacco shops and kiosks in central Stockholm. Additionally, some of the top hotels offer them on a complimentary basis.

The Stockholm Visitors Board publishes a guide to what is happening around the capital called *What's On?*. This is available free, on a monthly basis, from Sweden House, other tourist outlets and at hotels. For Swedish news in English, check out www.thelocal.se.

MONEY

Currency. Sweden's monetary unit is the krona (crown), plural kronor, that is divided into 100 öre and abbreviated to kr. Confusingly, Sweden, Denmark and Norway all use the kronor as their national currency, and to distinguish between them they are abbreviated as SEK, DKK and NOK, respectively. (For currency restrictions, *see page 134*).

Silver coins: 1 krona and 5 kronor. Golden coins: 10 kronor. Banknotes: 20, 50, 100, 500 and 1,000 kronor.

Banks and currency exchange. Foreign currency can be changed in all commercial and savings banks as well as in the larger hotels and department stores. FOREX, www.forex.se, has offices at Centralstationen (Central Station), the Arlanda Express Terminal, Arlanda Airport and throughout the city that are open daily and advertise that they offer the best exchange rate and lowest commission.

Credit cards and travellers' cheques. Most of the international credit cards are welcome; shops and restaurants usually display signs indicating the ones they accept. Travellers' cheques can be cashed at the bank or at your hotel. Credit card cancellation numbers: American Express 0771-29 56 00; Diners 08-14 68 78; for Mastercard, Eurocard or Visa, contact your bank.

VAT/sales tax. This is called Moms in Sweden, and is 25 percent on most goods and services (12 percent for accommodation). A 14–17.5 percent refund is available to non-EU residents on products valued at more than 200kr. Moms will be refunded in cash at any point of departure to visitors who have made purchases in shops displaying the blue-and-yellow 'Tax-Free Shopping' sticker. You should present your passport at the time of purchase. Later, simply hand over the tax-free shopping receipt provided by the shop (be sure to fill in the back), at the tax-free service counter in ports, airports and aboard ships. This refund is available only for a limited period after purchase and is only open to those who are not EU residents.

O

OPENING HOURS

Shops and department stores are usually open weekdays 10am– 6.30pm and Saturdays until 4pm. Department stores stay open later on weekdays and Saturdays and are open on Sunday afternoons. Food shops have longer hours and are also open on Sunday afternoons. Certain food shops (convenience stores), *närbutiker*, are open every day of the year from either 7am–11pm, or 10am–10pm.

Banks are generally open Mon–Fri 10am–3pm, with some in central Stockholm staying open until 5pm.

Museums are usually open Tue–Sun 10 or 11am to 4pm.

Chemists in Stockholm are generally open during normal shopping hours; a number stay open on duty at night and on Sundays *(see page 123)*.

P

POLICE *(polis)*

The Stockholm police patrol cars are marked 'Polis'. Members of the police force are invariably courteous and helpful to tourists and all of them speak at least some English, so don't hesitate to ask them any questions or directions. A police station is located in the Centralstationen (Central Station), Bryggargatan 19, tel: 08-401 0100.

The emergency police number (also fire, ambulance, etc) is **112**, and for non-emergencies it is **114 14**; no money is required when calling from a public pay phone.

There are traffic wardens, dressed in light-blue uniforms that check the time limits on the parking of cars and issue parking tickets for violations of the restrictions (they do a thorough job). On the motorways and major roads the police often carry out routine spot-checks.

POST OFFICES *(postkontor)*

The main post office is at Centralstationen (Central Station), tel: 08-781 24 25, Mon–Fri 7am–10pm, Sat–Sun 9am–6pm. Many grocery stores and corner shops (check 7-Eleven and Pressbyrån) also offer postal services. To receive your mail general delivery (poste restante) have it sent to the Central Post Office, Stockholm 11120. Post boxes can be found in the street – blue for local mail, yellow for non-local.

I want to send this by...	**Jag vill skicka det här...**
airmail	**med flyg**
express	**express**

PUBLIC HOLIDAYS *(helgdag)*

Banks, offices and shops close on public holidays in Sweden, as do most restaurants, museums, food shops and tourist attractions. Note that many establishments also close early on the day before a holiday – some may even close for the entire day beforehand. On Christmas Eve virtually everything is closed.

1 January	Nyårsdagen	New Year's Day
6 January	Trettondagen	Twelfth Day
1 May	Första Maj	May Day
Saturday between 20 and 26 June	Midsommardagen	Midsummer Day

Saturday between

31 Oct and 6 Nov	Allhelgonadagen	All Saints' Day
24 December	Julafton	Christmas Eve
25 December	Juldagen	Christmas Day
26 December	Annandag jul	Boxing Day

Movable Dates

late March/early April	Långfredagen	Good Friday
	Påskdagen/	Easter/
	Annandag påsk	Easter Monday
May	Kristi himmels-	
	färdsdag	Ascension Day
	Pingstdagen/	Whit Sunday/
	Annandag pingst	Monday

T

TELEPHONE *(telefon)*.

The country code for Sweden is 46. The city code for Stockholm is 08; the initial 0, though, is dropped when making an international call to Sweden. The 08 is dropped when calling within Stockholm, unless dialling from a mobile phone. Any number beginning with 020 indicates a toll-free call.

Predominantly, these days, phone booths take prepaid, disposable telephone cards that can be purchased at a minimum rate of 30kr from tourist offices, Pressbyrån and other kiosks. There are some booths, identified by a 'CCC' sign, that accept credit cards.

Remember, calling home – or anywhere else – from your hotel room is always prohibitively expensive unless, that is, you are using a calling card, or some other similar system, from your local long-distance supplier, in which case, find out from that supplier the free connection number applicable to the countries (they are different for each country) you are travelling to before you leave, as these numbers are not always easily available once there. Although dialling these numbers from public telephone booths is nominally toll-free, this is not as simple as it seems. It is not possible to connect from coin-operated booths without using a prepaid card, against which a small charge is made, to connect to the system before you can actually make a toll-free call. A bigger frustration may be finding a phone booth in a city where mobile phone usage is among the highest in the world.

Mobile phone roaming is possible in Stockholm, but charges are high. For longer stays and cheaper rates a local SIM card is the best option. Various outlets supply these, but a major centre is Phonehouse at Kungsgatan 29, tel: 08-11 03 50.

TIME ZONES

Sweden follows Central European Time (GMT + 1). In summer, the Swedes put their clocks ahead one hour. The following chart shows times across the world in summer:

New York	London	Paris	**Stockholm**	Sydney	Auckland
6am	11am	noon	**noon**	8pm	10pm

TIPPING

Service charges are included in hotel and restaurant bills. Gratuities for waiters, hotel maids, tourist guides and many others in the tourist-related industries are purely optional. Obviously, a little extra is appreciated for special services rendered, but it isn't expected. In some areas, however, the habit may be more ingrained:

Cloakroom attendant	charges posted
Hairdresser/barber	optional
Hotel porter, per bag	10kr
Taxi driver	optional to round up to the nearest ten
Waiter/waitress	around 10 percent of bill if satisfied

TOILETS *(toalett)*

Public facilities are located in some underground stations, department stores and some of the bigger streets, squares and parks. They are often labelled with symbols for men and women, or marked WC, Damer/Herrar (Ladies/Gentlemen) or simply D/H. Toilets are rarely free of charge, unless in a restaurant or café. Some have slots for coins or an attendant to give towels and soap. The usual charge is 5kr.

Where are the toilets?	**Var är toaletten?**

TOURIST INFORMATION

In Stockholm the main place to go is the **Tourist Centre** at Sweden House (Sverigehuset), Vasagatan 14, 111 20 Stockholm, tel: 08-508 28 508, www.visitstockholm.com; Mon–Fri 9am–7pm, Sat 10am–5pm, Sun 10am–4pm. This is the main tourist office in Stockholm and offers maps, books and other tourist information. You can buy tickets here for excursions, sightseeing and concerts, and book tour guides for individuals and groups *(see page 114)*. The tourist centre is also the home of the Sweden Shop, Sverige Shopen, for souvenirs and the FOREX foreign currency exchange office.

Hotellcentralen *(see page 103)* also provides tourist information.

The Sweden Bookshop with information about Sweden in foreign languages is found at Slottsbacken 10 by the Royal Palace.

The **Swedish Travel and Tourism Council** also has representatives in the following countries:

US: PO Box 4649, Grand Central Station, New York, NY, 10163-4649, tel: 212-885 9700, fax: 212-885 9710, www.visitsweden.com.
UK: Swedish Travel & Tourism Council, Sweden House, 5 Upper Montagu Street, London W1H 2AG, tel: 020-7724 5872, www.visit sweden.com.

The **Stockholm Card** *(Stockholmskortet)* offers you the chance to see the city at a reasonable price. It offers the holder free entry to 75 museums, castles and other attractions, plus free local public transport – including sightseeing boats, free city-centre street parking and more. Used to the full, the card represents a considerable bargain, and each adult can purchase up to two cards for children between the ages of 7 to 17. Its validity is for one, two, three or four days and costs 425kr and 195kr, 550kr and 225kr, 650kr and 245kr, 895kr and 285kr, for adults and children, respectively. These cards can be purchased at Sweden House, Hotellcentralen, some train stations, most tourist offices, campsites and youth hostels in and around Stockholm. More information about the Stockholm Card can be found at www.visitstockholm.com.

Throughout Sweden tourist offices *(turistbyrå)* are indicated by the international sign (a white 'i' on a green background). There are more than 300 non-profit tourist offices around the country. They stock a good selection of brochures and maps *(karta)* of their respective regions, and can provide you with information on sightseeing, excursions, restaurants, hotels, camping, sports, etc.

TRANSPORT

Bus, Subway and Local Trains. Stockholms Lokaltrafik (SL), tel: 08-600 10 00, www.sl.se, operates an extremely efficient bus, subway and commuter railway system that makes it easy to get around the city and its environs from about 5am (a little later on Sun) to 1am. The subway *(tunnelbana)* has over 100 stations that are indicated by a blue 'T' and are very creatively decorated, making them an attraction in their own right. There are maps for the underground in the station and on the train, and it is easy to get around on them.

Tickets can be bought at SL centres, local stations and any shops, such as Pressbyrån, that display the SL logo. There are ticket machines at some subway stations but you must have a ticket in advance before taking a bus as tickets cannot be bought on board.

On all public transport in Stockholm, children under 7 years of age travel free, while children between 7 and 18 pay half price.

Taxis. You can flag down taxis anywhere in Stockholm. Find them at stands marked 'Taxi', or call them by telephone. Taxi Stockholm, tel: 08-728 27 00, www.taxistockholm.se, is a well known firm, or check a local phone directory for numbers. Fares are metered.

Trains *(tåg)*. Swedish State Railway (Statens Järnvägar or S.J.), tel: 0771-75 75 75, www.sj.se, operates an extensive network of routes, with trains leaving Stockholm for most big towns every hour or two. The X2000 high-speed trains which can reach speeds of up to 200km/h (124mph) drastically cut the travelling times between Stockholm and other cities within the country. There are ticket machines at most stations, selling first and second class tickets.

Boat excursions. Stockholm and its environs are made-to-order for boat excursions. Sightseeing boats cruise under the city's bridges, steamers serve the islands of the archipelago in the Baltic and ply the waters of Lake Mälaren. Full details are available at Sweden House. The most popular short-hop boat trips are those from central Stockholm (Nybroviken) to the islands of Skeppsholmen and Djurgården. Tickets can be bought at the kiosk on the quayside or are included in the Stockholm Card. Strömma Kanalbolaget run cruises in the Stockholm archipelago: www.stromma.se.

How much is the fare to ...?	**Hur mycket kostar det till ...?**
Take me to this address.	**Kör mig till den här adressen.**
I'd like a	**Jag skulle vilja ha en**
ticket to...	**biljett till...**
single (one way)	**enkel**
return (round trip)	**tur och retur**
When is the ... train	**När går tåget**
to Uppsala?	**till Uppsala?**
first/last/next	**första/sista/nästa**
Will you tell me	**Kan ni säga till när**
when to get off?	**jag skall stiga av?**

VISAS AND ENTRY REQUIREMENTS (tull)

Visitors from EU countries need only an identity card to enter Sweden. Citizens of most other countries must be in possession of a valid passport, while South African citizens need a visa. Contact the Embassy of Sweden, 1166 Park Street, PO Box 13477, Hatfield 0028, South Africa, tel: 27-12 4266 400, fax: 27-12 4266 464, www.swedenabroad.com. European and North American residents are not subject to any health requirements. In case of doubt, check with Swedish representatives in your own country before departure.

Duty-free allowance. As Sweden is part of the EU, free exchange of non-duty-free goods for personal use is permitted between Sweden and other EU countries. Due to the high prices of alcohol and tobacco visitors might consider bringing in some of their own. If so, each person over 20 is allowed 1 litre of spirits (over 22 percent by volume) and those over 15 may carry with them 200 cigarettes.

Currency restrictions. There is no restriction on the amount of foreign or local currency you may bring into or take out of the country as a tourist (provided it is declared upon entry).

WEBSITES

The Stockholm Visitors Board maintains the very wide-ranging and informative site **www.visitstockholm.com**, which is readable in eight languages. Destination Stockholm, **www.destination-stockholm.com**, is dedicated to the Stockholm package of hotel accommodation and the Stockholm Card. The city of Stockholm operates the site **www.stockholm.se/english**, which has technical information about the city government, business information and useful links.

General, useful information about Sweden and also about the cities of Stockholm, Göteborg and Malmö can be found at

www.visitsweden.com. Information about Uppsala can be found at **www.uppsala.se**. Swedish news in English and other general information can be found at **www.thelocal.se**.

Y

YOUTH HOSTELS (vandrarhem)

The Stockholm Visitors Board publishes a booklet on hotels and youth hostels in Stockholm that also lists hostels in the archipelago and around Lake Mälaren. Hostelling International, tel: 01707-324 170, www.hihostels.com, also lists hostels around Sweden. You should expect to pay between 60–300kr per night, with breakfast and sheets extra.

The following are some recommended youth hostels in Stockholm:

Af Chapman & Skeppsholmen Flaggmansvägen 8, Skeppsholmen, SE-111 49, tel: 08-463 22 66, www.sftchapman.com. Located in a landmark 1888 ship, with additional accommodation on shore, this hostel has a spectacular view of Gamla Stan. Advance reservations recommended during summer. Open all year. Dorm beds from 260kr, rooms from 560kr.

City Backpackers Upplandsgatan 2A, SE-111 23, tel: 08-20 69 20, www.citybackpackers.se. In a 19th-century building, and within walking distance of Gamla Stan, this offers rooms with between 1 to 12 beds. Dorms start from 109kr.

Hotel Renstierna Renstiernas Gata 15, SE-116 28, tel: 08-615 21 35, www.hotelrenstierna.se. Centrally located on Södermalm with clean and modern facilities. 11 rooms. Prices start from 550kr.

Långholmens Vandrarhem Långholmsmuren 20, Box 9116, SE-102 72, tel: 08-720 85 00, www.langholmen.com. This is an excellent hostel on the island of Långholmen, located within an old prison building. Accommodation in 'cells' with two to four bunkbeds. Most have their own shower and wc. Restaurant and café on the premises. Bathing beach. Prices start from 260kr.

Recommended Hotels

The price categories below are based on two people sharing a double room at full rates, including breakfast, Moms (sales tax at 12 percent), and service charge. However, there are usually substantial discounts for weekends and during the summer season. Major credit cards are accepted everywhere.

You can also book rooms through Hotellcentralen (the Hotel Centre, Central Station, tel: 08-508 285 08, www.visitstockholm.com), Stockholm's official tourist accommodation agency. The following is a list of selected accommodation divided into four price categories.

€€€€	over 2,200kr
€€€	1,500–2,200kr
€€	1,000–1,500kr
€	below 1,000kr

MODERN STOCKHOLM

Adlon Hotell €€€ *Vasagatan 42, SE-111 20, tel: 08-402 65 00, www.adlon.se.* Established in 1944, this hotel, close to Central Station, has always been privately owned and independently run. A designated IT hotel, your room can become your office. 83 rooms.

Berns Hotel €€€€ *Näckströmsgatan 8, SE-111 47, tel: 08-566 320 00, www.berns.se.* Small, intimate and exclusive hotel with rooms of varying sizes – one has its own sauna. All rooms have a distinguished contemporary décor designed around rich marble and cherry wood. 65 rooms.

Best Western Kom Hotel €€ *Döbelnsgatan 17, SE-11 40, tel: 08-412 23 00, www.komhotel.se.* The slightly bleak exterior gives way to a rather stylish interior, but this is a functional option with good location and facilities including a gym. 150 rooms.

Elite Hotel Stockholm Plaza €€€ *Birger Jarlsgatan 29, Box 7707, SE-103 28, tel: 08-566 220 00, www.elite.se.* An unusual 19th-century façade fronts a hotel with a pleasing atmosphere. Good location, very close to Stureplan. 151 rooms.

First Hotel Amaranten €€€€ *Kungsholmsgatan 31, SE-104 20, tel: 08-692 52 00, www.firsthotels.se.* This is a large, modern hotel with bags of style that also features a spa, and is found in a neat area just a short walk from City Hall and Central Station. 423 rooms.

Grand Hôtel Stockholm €€€€ *S. Blaiseholmshamnen 8, PO Box 16424, SE-103 27, tel: 08-679 35 00, www.grandhotel.se.* Grand in size, architecture, style and graciousness, the Grand is the only hotel of its class in Sweden. Fantastic views across to the Royal Palace in Gamla Stan, and a Michelin starred restaurant. 310 rooms.

Hotell Anno 1647 €€€ *Mariagränd 3, SE-116 41, tel: 08-442 16 80, www.anno1647.se.* Dating from 1647, this hotel retains its old-world charm and is located in a historic setting at Slussen. Close to Gamla Stan and the ferry to Djurgården. 42 rooms.

Hotell August Strindberg €€–€€€ *Tegnergatan 38, Se-113 59, tel: 08-32 50 06, www.hotellstrindberg.se.* Named after the national author and artist whose statue is in the nearby park. Clean and comfortable rooms, all en suite. 27 rooms.

Hotel Bema €€ *Upplandsgatan 13, SE-111 23, tel: 08-23 26 75, www.hotelbema.se.* Stockholm doesn't have a great deal of budget accommodation but this two-star hotel is a good option, well located with a pretty courtyard garden. 12 rooms, all with ensuite bathrooms.

Hotel Bentleys €€–€€€ *Drottninggattan 77, SE-111 60, tel: 08-14 13 95, www.bentleys.se.* Found in a house dating from the turn of the 20th century, and located at the top, and quieter, end of this famous shopping street, the Hotel Bentleys is a charming mid-size hotel that was completely renovated in 2010. All the rooms are individually designed. 119 rooms.

Hotel Birger Jarl €€€–€€€€ *Tulegatan 8, Box 19016, SE-104 32, tel: 08-674 18 00, www.birgerjarl.se.* The only hotel in Stockholm with a Swedish designer profile, this has been enhanced by the addition of business rooms and speciality rooms on the 7th floor created by different designers. 235 rooms. Sauna and gym.

Hotel Diplomat €€€€ *Strandvägen 7C, Box 14059, SE-104 40, tel: 08-459 68 00, www.diplomathotel.com.* A delightful Jugend-style building dating from 1911. Family owned, it has individually designed rooms and special business suites. Fine waterfront location. 128 rooms.

Hotel Esplanade €€€€ *Strandvägen 7A, SE-114 56, tel: 08-663 07 40, www.hotelesplanade.se.* Behind an attractive Jugend façade, this is a small, charming hotel containing individually decorated rooms. Views over Nybroviken Bay. 34 rooms.

Hotel Hellsten €€–€€€ *Luntmakargatan 68, SE-113 51, tel: 08-661 86 00, www.hellsten.se.* Located in a very trendy area, this is a hip hotel where each of the rooms – there are six different categories – has its own style, colour, textile design and furnishings. The junior suites are noted for their beautiful porcelain stoves and stuccoed ceilings. Seven of the rooms have balconies. A great hotel, large rooms and excellent value for money. 78 rooms.

Hotell Kung Carl €€€ *Birger Jarlsgatan 21, Box 1776, SE-111 87, tel: 08-463 50 00, www.hkchotels.se.* A historic hotel, now part of the Best Western chain, but that doesn't mean it's impersonal. Rooms vary from the traditional to the trendy. A fine, central location at Stureplan. 112 rooms.

Hotel Norrtull €€ *St Eriksgatan 119, SE-102 34, tel: 08-300 350, www.hotelnorrtull.se.* Located in a former 1920s wine warehouse, the Norrtull has been stylishly converted into a modern hotel, with wooden floors, Persian carpets and crisp white linen. 129 rooms.

Hotel Oden €€€ *Karlbergsvägen 24, SE-102 34, tel: 08-457 97 00, www.hoteloden.se.* Good value for money. Basic rooms, all of which have been refurbished over the past few years, with parquet floors replacing carpets. All have a fridge and some have a kitchenette. Solarium, sauna and exercise room. 140 rooms.

Hotel Tegnérlunden €€€ *Tegnérlunden 8, SE-113 59, tel: 08-545 455 50, www.hoteltegnerlunden.se.* Located in a quiet square just off the pedestrian shopping street of Drottninggatan and a few minutes' walk from Central Station. Wheelchair-friendly, rooftop breakfast room and sauna. 102 rooms.

Hotel Terminus €€€ *Vasagatan 20, Box 271, SE-101 25, tel: 08-440 16 70, www.terminus.se.* A Best Western hotel directly across from Central Station. Comfortable, traditional atmosphere. Recreation centre with sauna, jacuzzi and tanning bed. 155 rooms.

Långholmens Vandrarhem €€ *Långholmsmuren 20, Box 9116, SE-102 72, tel: 08-720 85 00, www.langholmen.com.* On the island of Långholmen, this was built as a prison in the early 19th century, closed in 1975, then converted to an unusual hotel and hostel 14 years later. Expect small rooms. 102 rooms.

Nordic Light Hotel €€€€ *Vasaplan 7, SE-101 37, tel: 08-505 630 00, www.nordiclighthotel.se.* Located next to the Arlanda Express rail link at Central Station, the hotel uses a unique lighting design which provides it with a truly Scandinavian feel. All the rooms have a contemporary style along with all modern facilities. 175 rooms.

Nordic Sea Hotel €€€ *Vasaplan 2–4, SE-101 37, tel: 08-505 630 00, www.nordicseahotel.se.* This hotel is situated across the road from its sister hotel, Nordic Light. Inspired by the sea, an element strongly associated with the Nordic countries, the hotel has a rugged, close-to-nature atmosphere combined with all modern facilities. It is also home to the famous Ice Bar, made of pure ice and maintained at 5°C (23°F), where you can have a drink from a 'glass' made of ice. 367 rooms.

Radisson Blu Royal Viking Hotel €€€ *Vasagatan 1, Box 234, SE-101 24, tel: 08-50 65 40 00, www.radissonblu.com/royalvikinghotel-stockholm.* A conveniently located hotel next to Central Station and airport buses. The Bermuda Pool Club has a pool, whirlpool, sauna, massage and gym. Wireless broadband internet access is available. Excellent fish restaurant and rooftop bar. 459 rooms.

Radisson Blu SkyCity Hotel €€–€€€ *Sky City, SE-190 45 Stockholm-Arlanda, tel: 08-506 740 00, www.radissonblu.com/sky cityhotel-stockholmairport*. Located in the Arlanda Airport and SkyCity complex. 230 rooms.

Radisson Blu Strand Hotel €€€€ *Nybrokajen 9, Box 16396, SE-103 27, tel: 08-50 66 40 00, www.radissonblu.com/strandhotel-stockholm*. Large, traditional, ivy-covered building overlooking the boats on Nybroviken Bay. Business-class suites available. 24-hour room service and sauna. 152 rooms.

Rex Hotel €€€ *Luntmakargatan 73, SE-113 51, tel: 08-16 00 40, www.rexhotel.se*. In a building dating from 1866, just across from its sister hotel, the Hellsten. The rooms' attractive design is based on the use of muted greys and beiges, accented with occasional strong colours. The entrance is through a brick-vaulted gate leading to a charming garden where breakfast is served in the warmer months. 32 rooms.

Rica City Hotel Kungsgatan €€€ *Kungsgatan 47, SE-111 56, tel: 08-723 72 20, www.rica.cityhotels.se, www.rica.se/hotelkungsgatan*. A large city-centre hotel with classic Swedish minimalist design. Located above the PUB department store. 270 rooms.

Scandic Hotel Anglais €€€€ *Humlegårdsgatan 23, SE-102 44, tel: 08-517 340 00, www.scandichotels.com*. A modern hotel, opposite Humlegården Park and just a short walk to Stureplan and the city centre. 230 rooms.

Scandic Hotel Continental €€€–€€€€ *Vasagatan/Klar Vatugränd 4, SE-101 22, tel: 08-517 342 00, www.scandichotels.com*. Located in the city centre across from Central Station. Business centre and conference rooms. 268 rooms.

Scandic Sergel Plaza Hotel €€€ *Brunkebergstorg 9, SE-103 27, tel: 08-517 263 00, www.scandichotels.com*. Located in a central position just behind Sergels Torg and the Kulturhuset. A distinguished hotel with a charming lobby, piano bar, pool, fitness centre and 24-hour room service. 403 rooms.

Sheraton Stockholm Hotel & Towers €€€–€€€€ *Tegelbacken 6, SE-101 23, tel: 08-412 34 00, www.sheratonstockholm.com.* Near the Central Station and with fine views over Lake Mälaren, Gamla Stan and City Hall. Large rooms and suites. Three restaurants, fitness centre, casino and sauna. 462 rooms.

GAMLA STAN (OLD TOWN)

First Hotel Reisen €€€–€€€€ *Skeppsbron 12, SE-111 30, tel: 08-22 32 60, www.firsthotels.com.* A nicely located and beautifully designed 19th-century hotel on the Gamla Stan waterfront, overlooking Skeppsholmen. Sauna, pool and piano bar. 144 rooms.

Lady Hamilton Hotel €€€ *Storkyrkobrinken 5, SE-111 28, tel: 08-506 401 00, www.thecollectorshotels.se/lady-hamilton.* This Class-A listed building dates from the late 15th century. Expect nautical memorabilia and antiques – including a collection of grandfather clocks. Take a dip in an early 14th-century well in the basement. 30 rooms.

Lord Nelson Hotel €€€ *Vasterlånggatan 22, SE-111 29, tel: 08-506 101 20, www.thecollectorshotels.se/lord nelson.* A 17th century building in Gamla Stan with a width of less than 5m (16ft), making it Sweden's narrowest hotel. A nautical flavour throughout. Fairly small newly renovated rooms. 30 rooms.

Rica Hotel Gamla Stan €€€ *Lilla Nygatan 25, SE-110 28, tel: 08-723 72 50, www.rica-hotels.com.* A converted 17th-century house at the southern end of the Gamla Stan. Quiet and tucked away among the narrow streets, all rooms have been renovated to a high standard in an 18th-century Gustavian style. 51 rooms.

Victory Hotel €€€ *Lilla Nygatan 5, SE-111 28, tel: 08-506 400 00, www.thecollectorshotels.se/en/victory.* A 17th-century residence in Gamla Stan now a small, intimate Relais & Chateaux hotel, named after Lord Nelson's flagship. Rooms individually decorated with antiques. Bar, sauna and an excellent restaurant. 45 rooms.

RIDDARHOLMEN

Hotell Mälardrottningen € *Riddarholmen, SE-111 28, tel: 08-545 187 80, www.malardrottningen.se.* One of Stockholm's most unusual hotels. A 1920s' luxury yacht formerly owned by American millionairess Barbara Hutton, now anchored at Riddarholmen – next to Gamla Stan (see page 34). The cabins have been converted into hotel rooms. 61 rooms.

SÖDERMALM

Hilton Stockholm Slussen €€€€ *Guldgränd 8, SE-104 65, tel: 08-517 353 00, www.hilton.com.* An impressive modern hotel with spacious, well-equipped rooms, many of which offer spectacular views over the waters of Riddarfjärden to Gamla Stan and City Hall. It also features two restaurants and bars, a wine cellar, and a fitness centre with sauna as well as a chiropractic clinic. 289 rooms.

Hotel Tre Små Rum € *Högbergsgatan 81, SE-118 54, tel: 08-641 23 71, www.tresmarum.se.* A small bed and breakfast hotel located in Södermalm. To get there, take the Red Line, destination Norsborg/Fruängen. Alternatively, alight at stop Mariatorget on the 'T' (metro). Organic breakfast. 7 rooms.

Rival Hotel €€€ *Mariatorget 3, SE-118 91, tel: 08-545 789 00, www.rival.se.* This, Stockholm's first boutique hotel (owned by Benny Andersson, formerly of Abba), is found in an historical building that used to be the home of the Rival Cinema. The cinematic theme is evident in all the rooms – in fact the hotel still has a cinema screen. Features include open-plan bedrooms and bathrooms and 32-inch plasma TVs complete with DVD/CD players. 99 rooms.

UPPSALA

Clarion Hotel Gillet €€€–€€€€ *Dragarbrunnsgatan 23, SE-751 42, tel: 018-68 18 00, www.clarionhotelgillet.se.* An excellent location in the centre of town. Pool, sauna and excellent restaurant. 160 rooms and 23 conference rooms.

INDEX

Berlitz pocket guide

Stockholm

Seventh Edition 2012

Written by Norman Renouf
Updated by Zoe Ross
Commissioned by Rebecca Lovell
Series Editor: Tom Stainer

Photography credits
All photography by Julian Love/APA except Pål
Allan/Swedish Institute 102; Louise Billgert 87;
Alexander V. Dokukin/Stockholm Visitors Board
(SVB) 38; Lars Ekdahl/Millesgarden 3BL, 6B, 64; Ola
Ericson/imagebank.sweden.se 6T, 10, 14, 91; Tuukka
Ervasti/imagebank.sweden.se 4TL, 7T, 82, 85; Mans
Fornander/imagebank.sweden.se 96; Olof
Holdar/SVB 37, 86; Jan Lindblad Jr/APA 10, 17, 33,
45, 56, 57, 58, 59, 63, 65, 75, 76; Maria Ljunggren/the
National Maritime Museum 61; Moderna Museet 46;
Theresia Parsby 89; Maria Rundquist/The Royal
Court of Sweden 24; Swedish Tourist Board 22

Cover picture: José Fuste Raga/Zefa/Corbis

Every effort has been made to provide
accurate information in this publication,
but changes are inevitable. The publisher
cannot be responsible for any resulting
loss, inconvenience or injury.

Contact us

At Berlitz we strive to keep our guides as
accurate and up to date as possible, but if you
find anything that has changed, or if you have
any suggestions on ways to improve this guide,
then we would be delighted to hear from you.

Berlitz Publishing, PO Box 7910,
London SE1 1WE, England.
email: berlitz@apaguide.co.uk
www.berlitzpublishing.com